AF609456

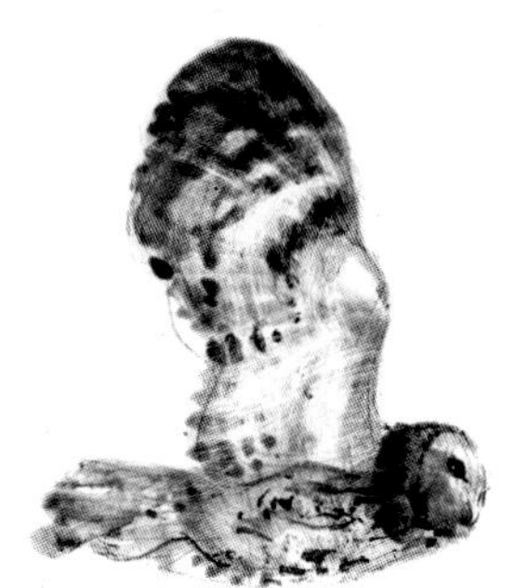

Darkling

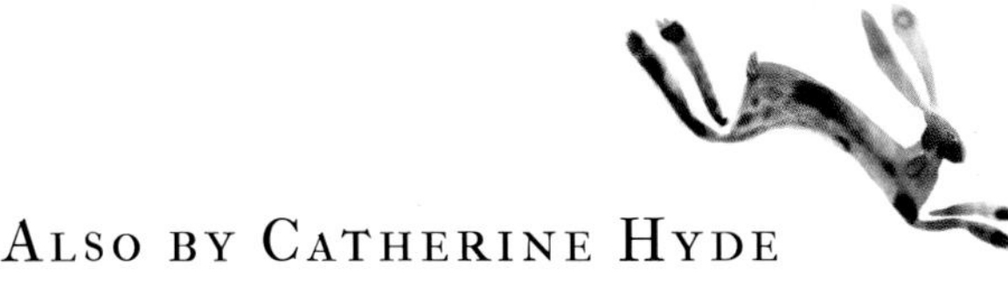

ALSO BY CATHERINE HYDE

The Hare and the Moon

The Bee and the Sun

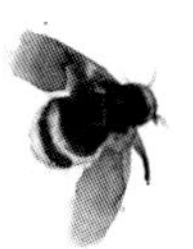

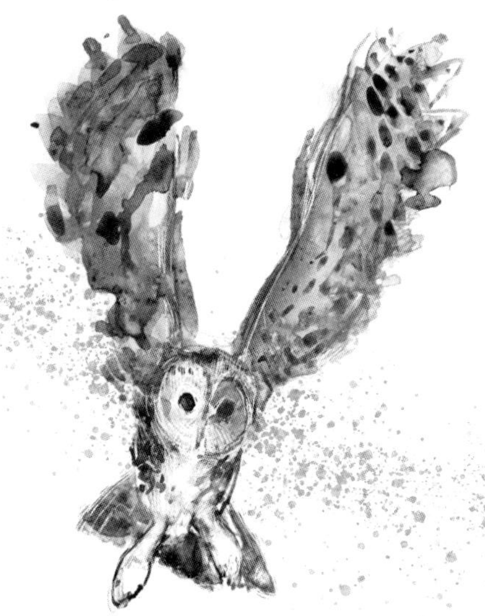

DARKLING

The Owl's Song

CATHERINE HYDE

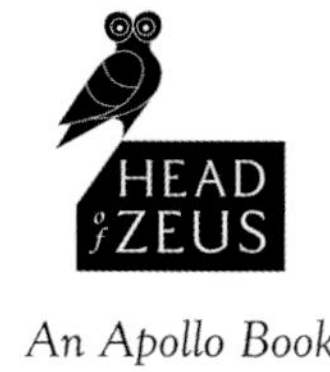

An Apollo Book

First published in the UK in 2024 by Head of Zeus Ltd,
part of Bloomsbury Publishing Plc

9 7 5 3 1 2 4 6 8

A CIP catalogue record for this book is available from the British Library.

ISBN (HB): 9781035900961
ISBN (E): 9781035900954

Designed by Jessie Price

Printed and bound in China by C&C Offset Printing Co., Ltd.

Head of Zeus Ltd
First Floor East
5–8 Hardwick Street
London EC1R 4RG
www.headofzeus.com

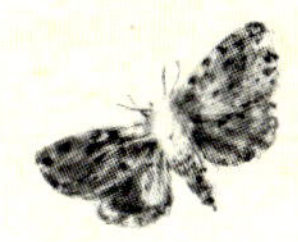

For my dearest and ever patient
friends and family and all who love
the calling of the owls.

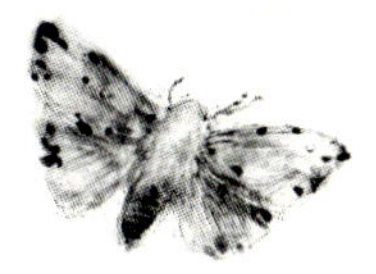

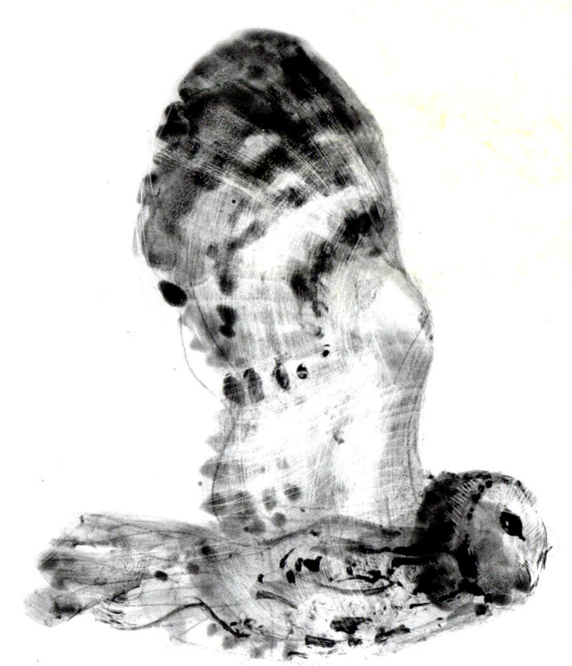

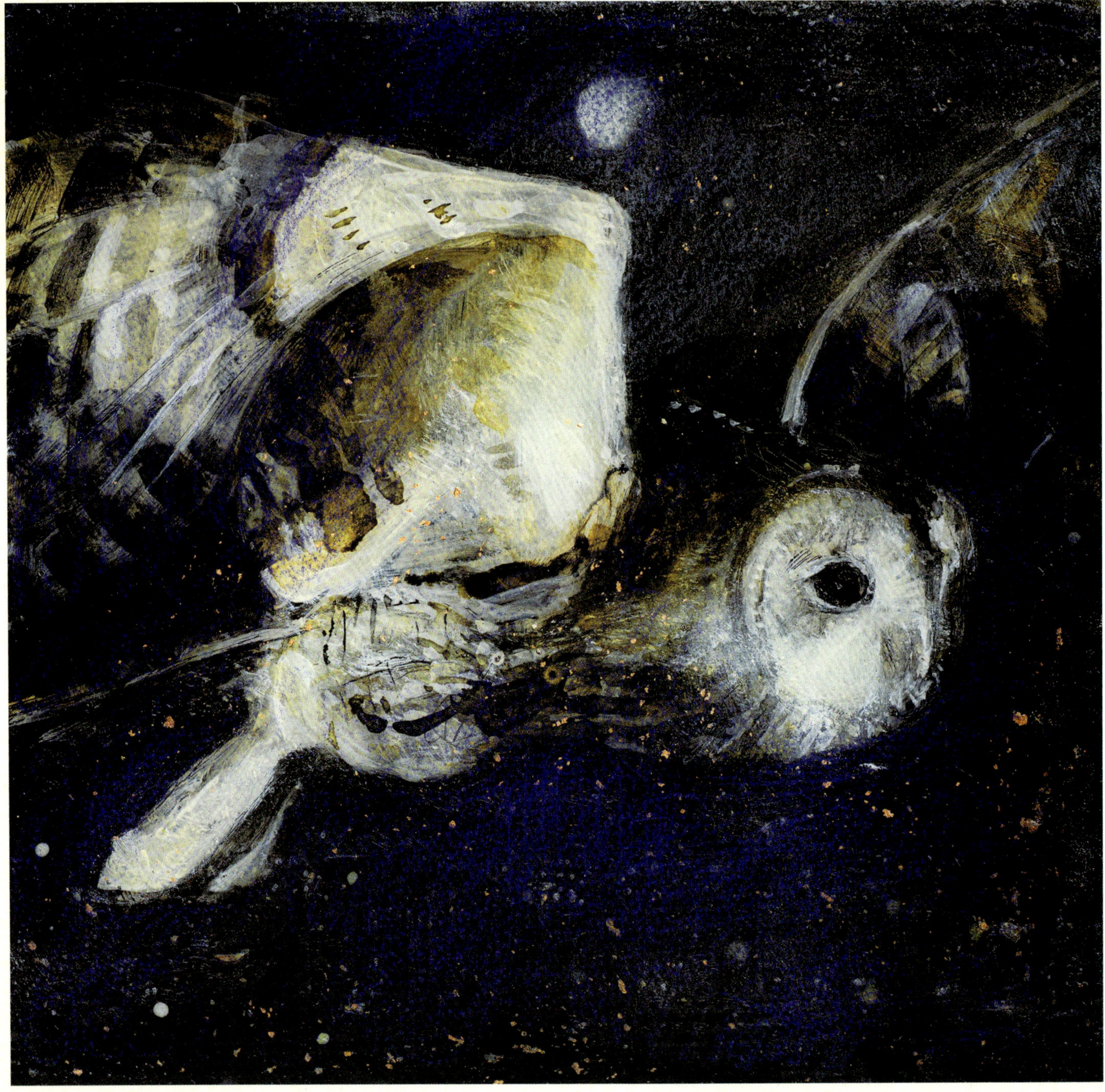

I am the silence before day's dawning,
the hooting that conjures night.
I am the charm that promises luck,
the portent that takes it away.
I am the spirit that lives in the oak
and I am the darkling at the end of the day.

I sit
and I call twilight to me.

In the distance,
she answers
Kee witt
Kee witt

I sit.
And I listen.
I sit,
and I
watch.

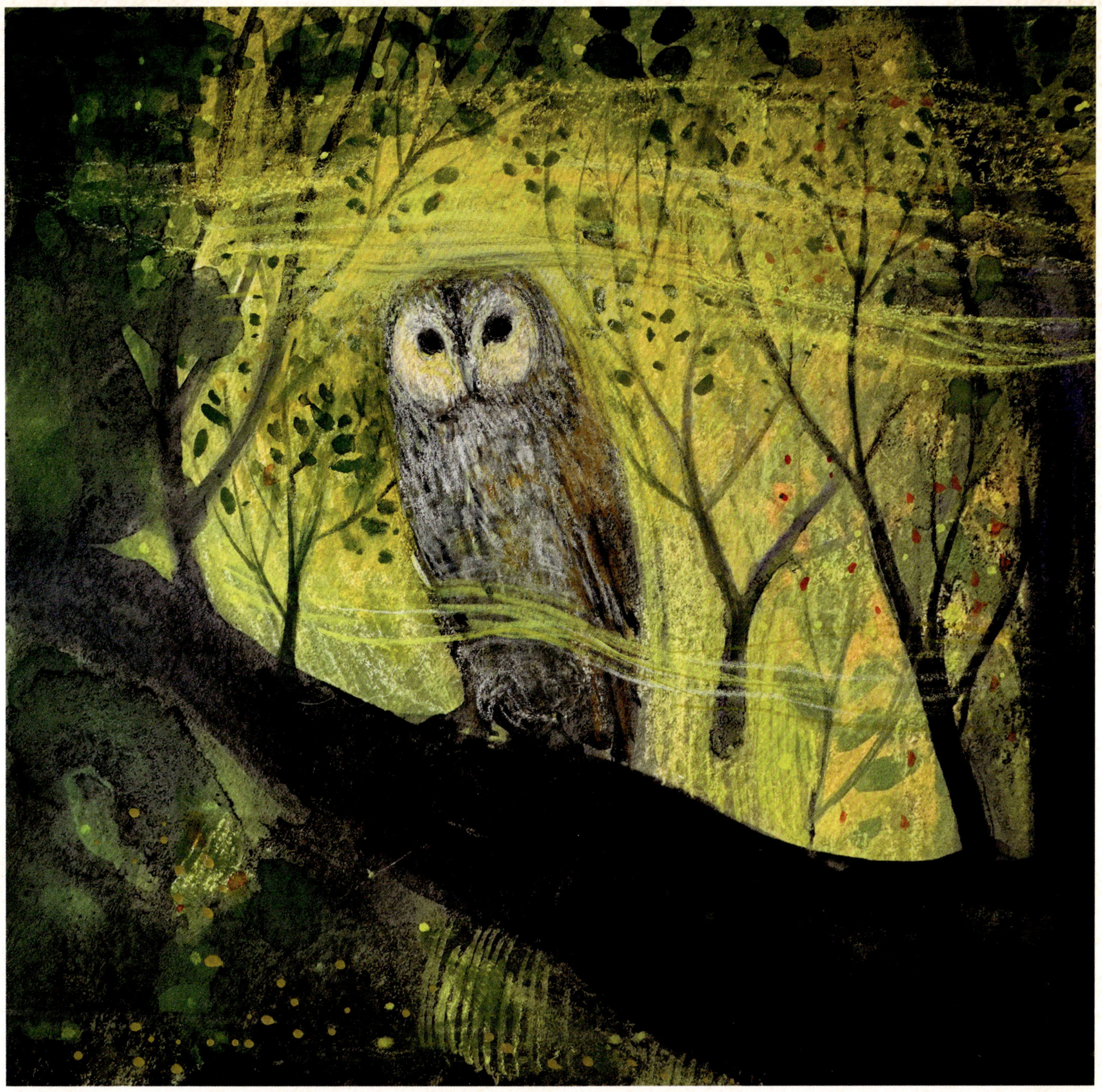

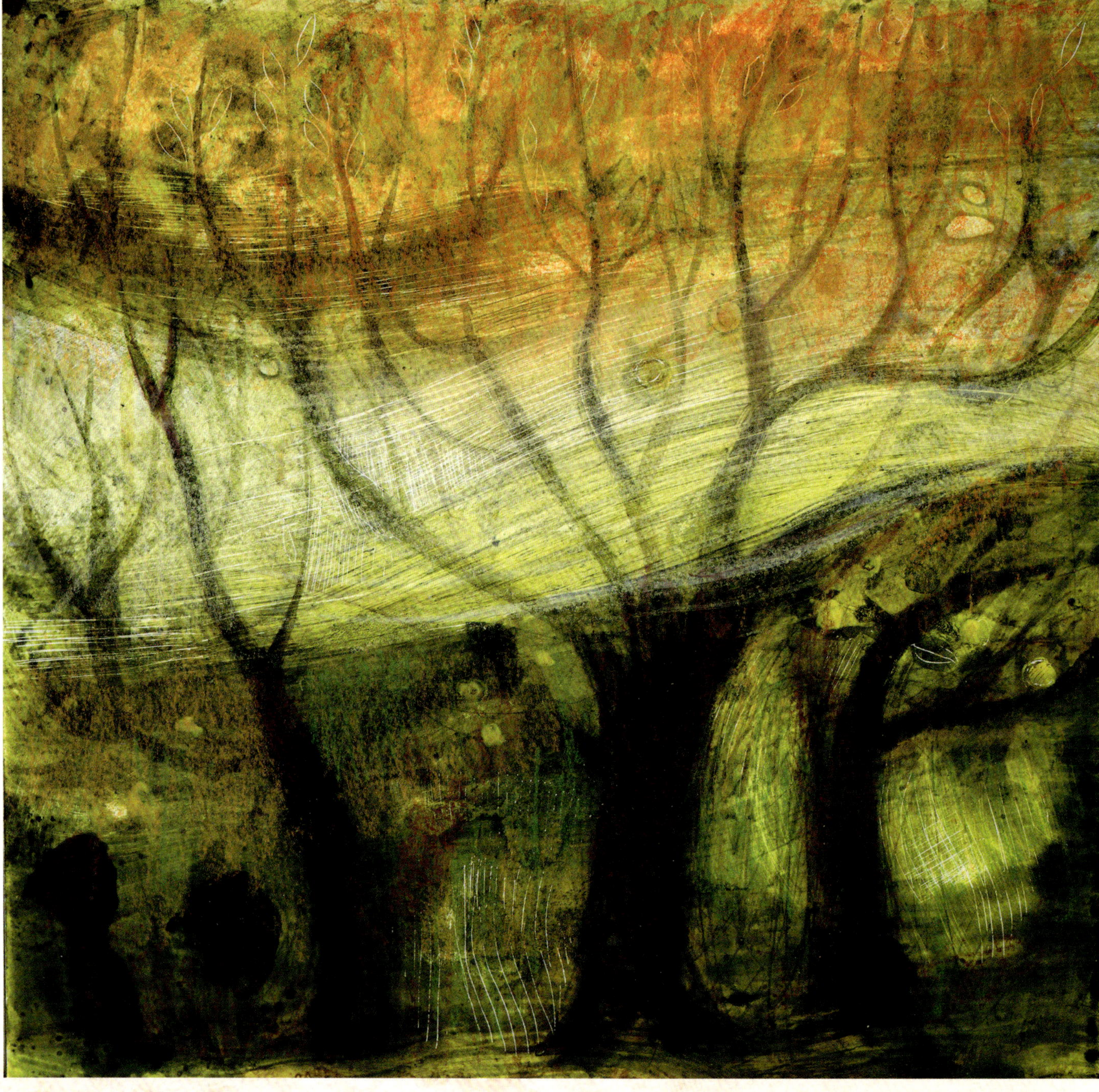

In the Darkling Wood
day's light is fading
into hazy uncertainty.
Coiled on the breeze,
leafy woodsmoke
drifts.
Shadows lengthen,
creeping like ink
into hawthorn and holly.

Among the apple trees
a mistle-thrush sings.
Wood pigeons call.

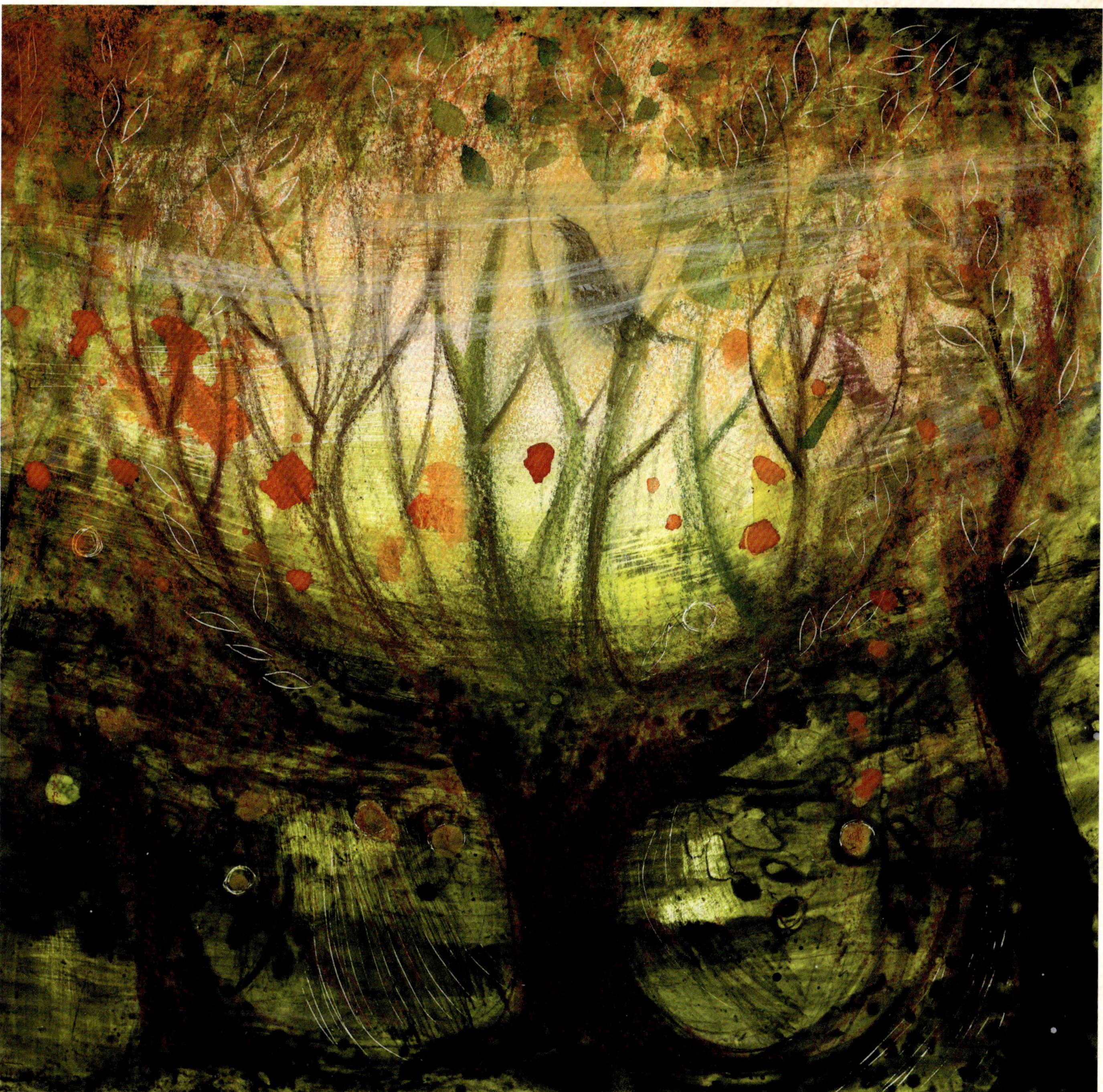

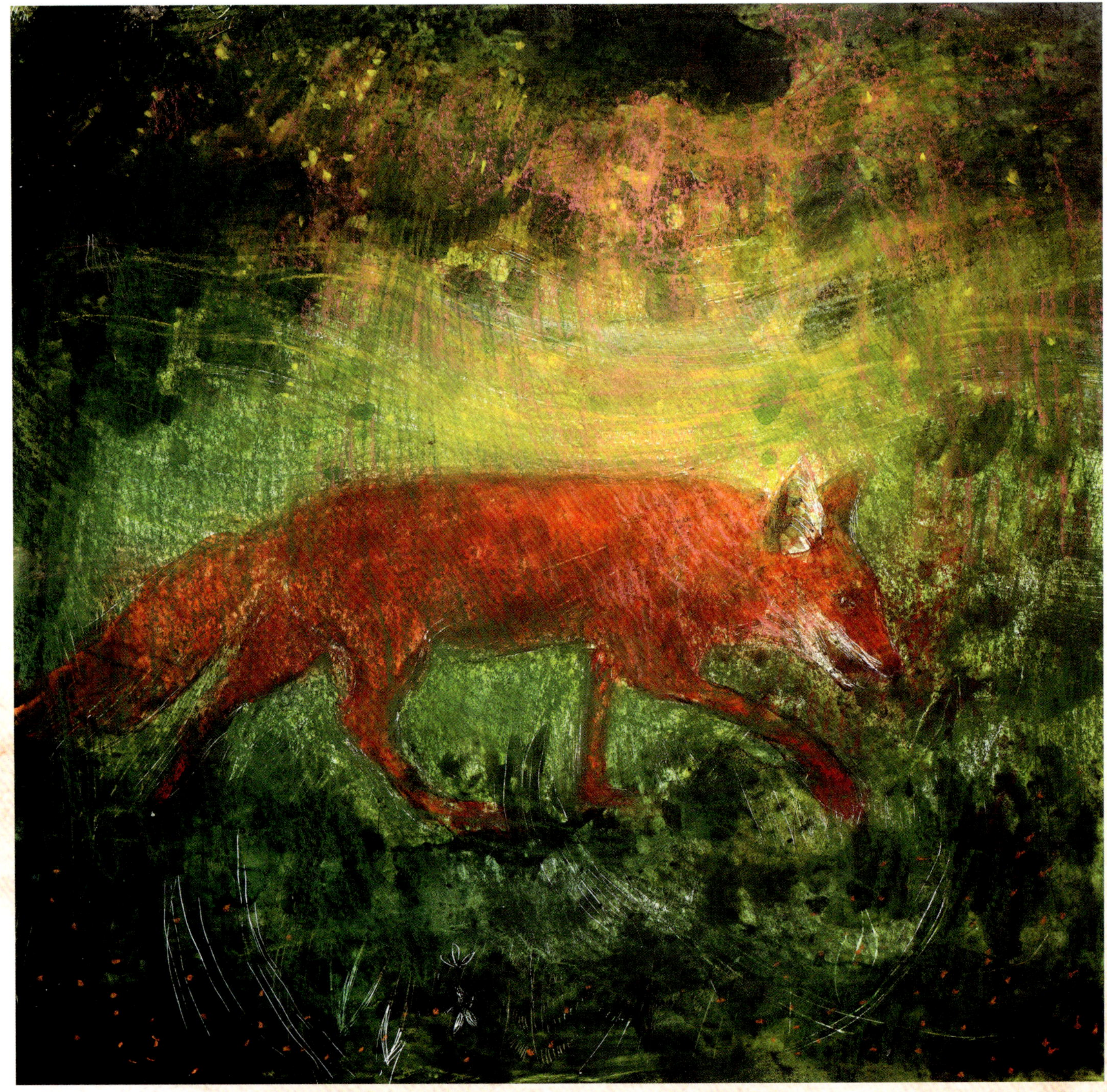

Fox
tiptoes into dissolving light,
vixen red in darker green,

I listen:

to rustling below,
scurrying,
ruffling leaf litter.

I drop:
make a killing.

Blackbird chucks, alarmed.
A chatter of sparrows explodes,
then settles,
quiet in the deep hedge.

Stillness.

Swallows group,
and swoop
away.

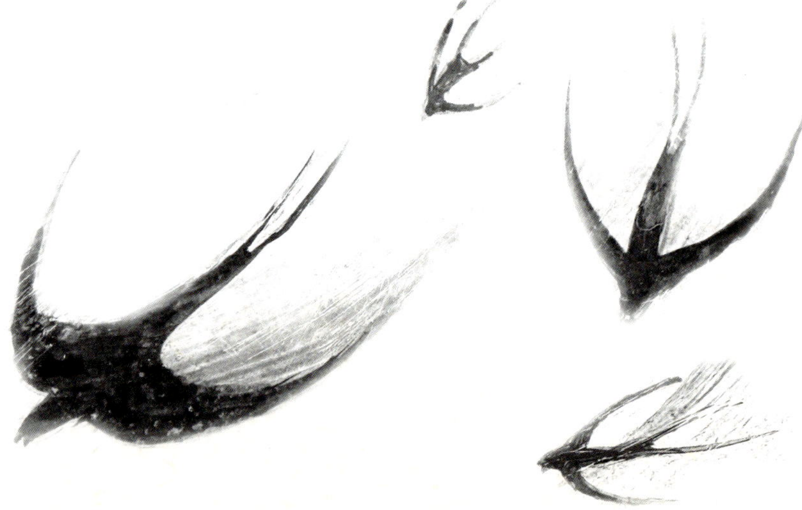

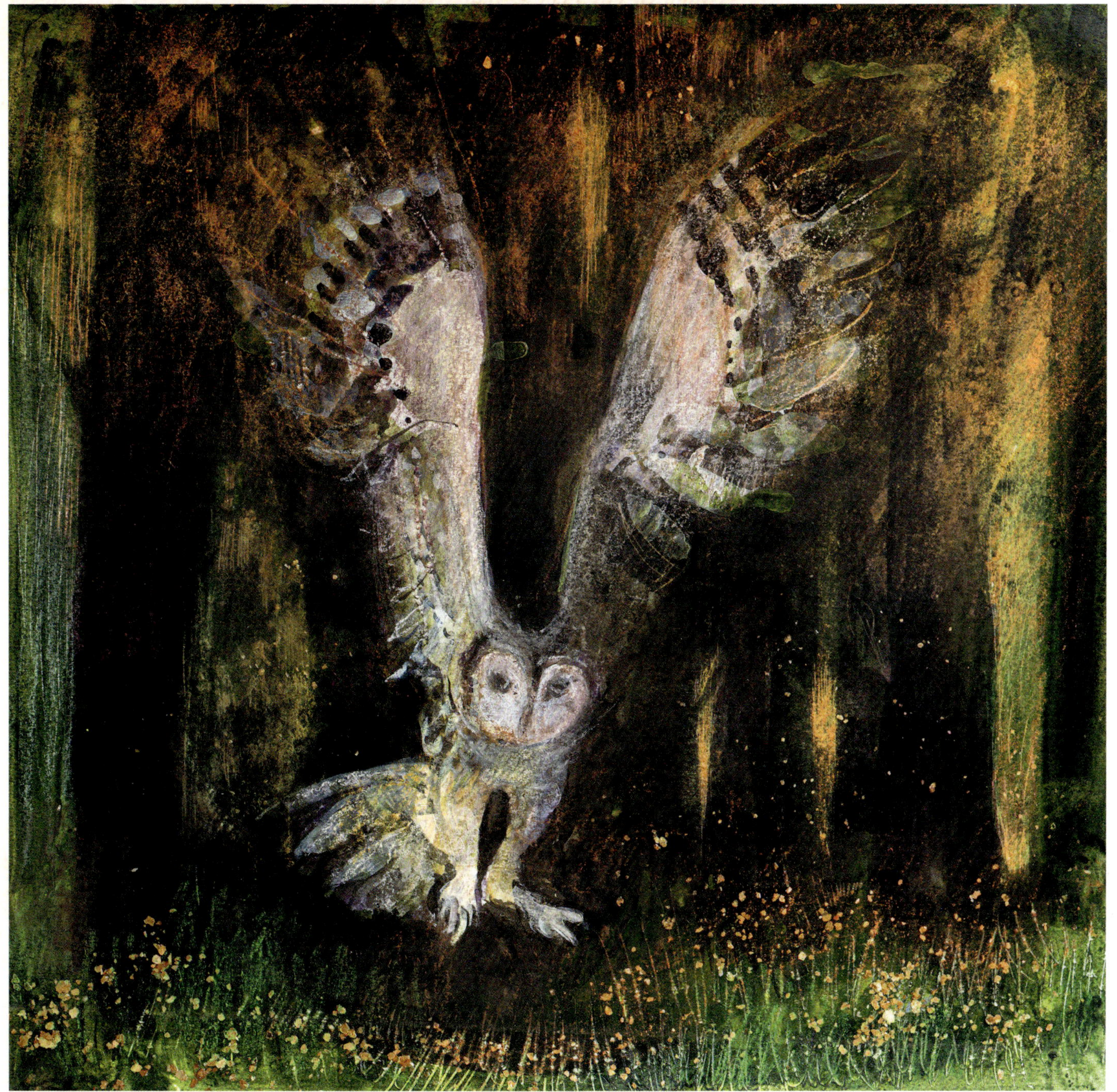

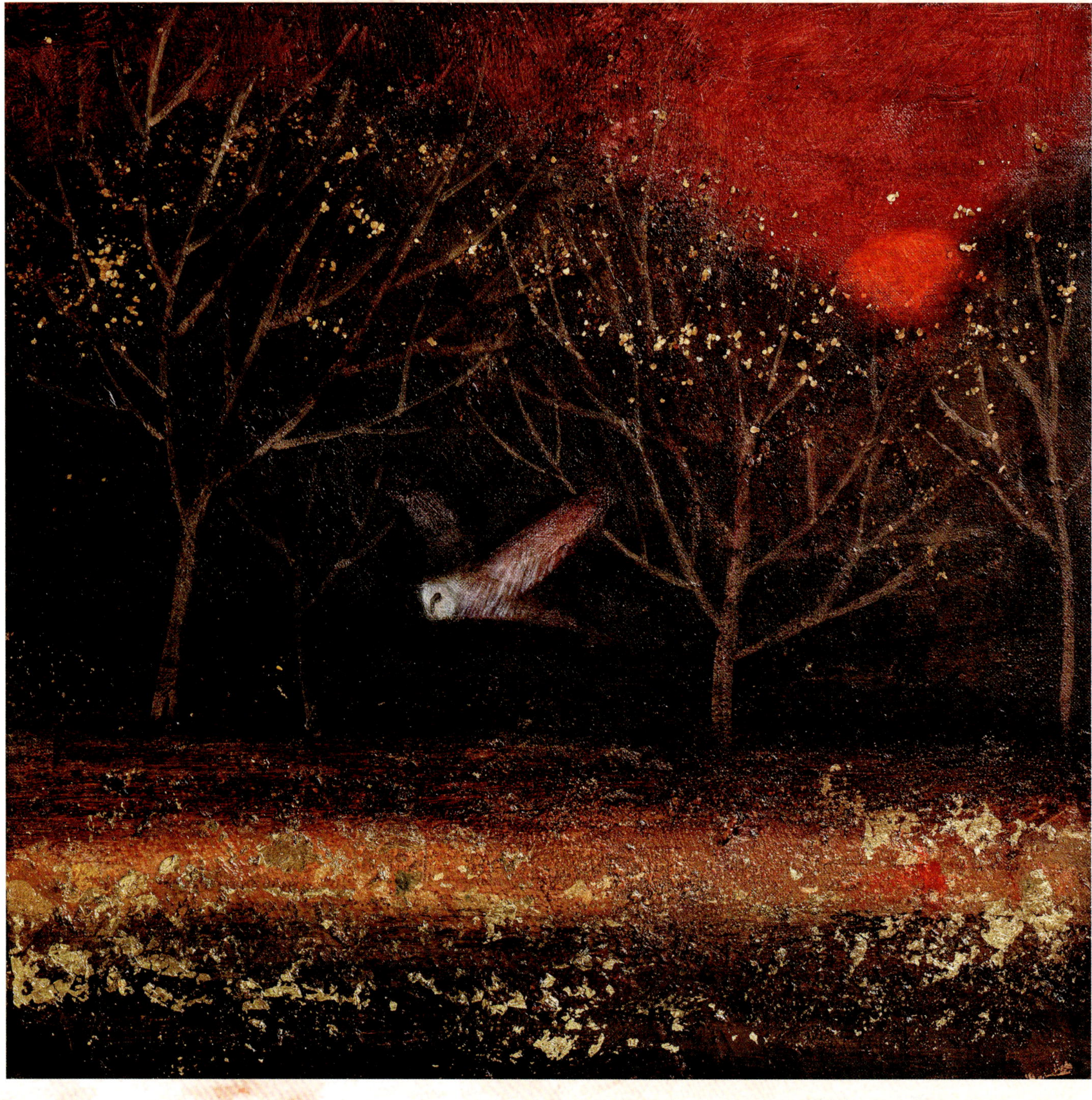

In the distance,
she answers
Kee witt
Kee witt

The wind turns,
promising rain.

The last moments of day linger,
sky glows gold.

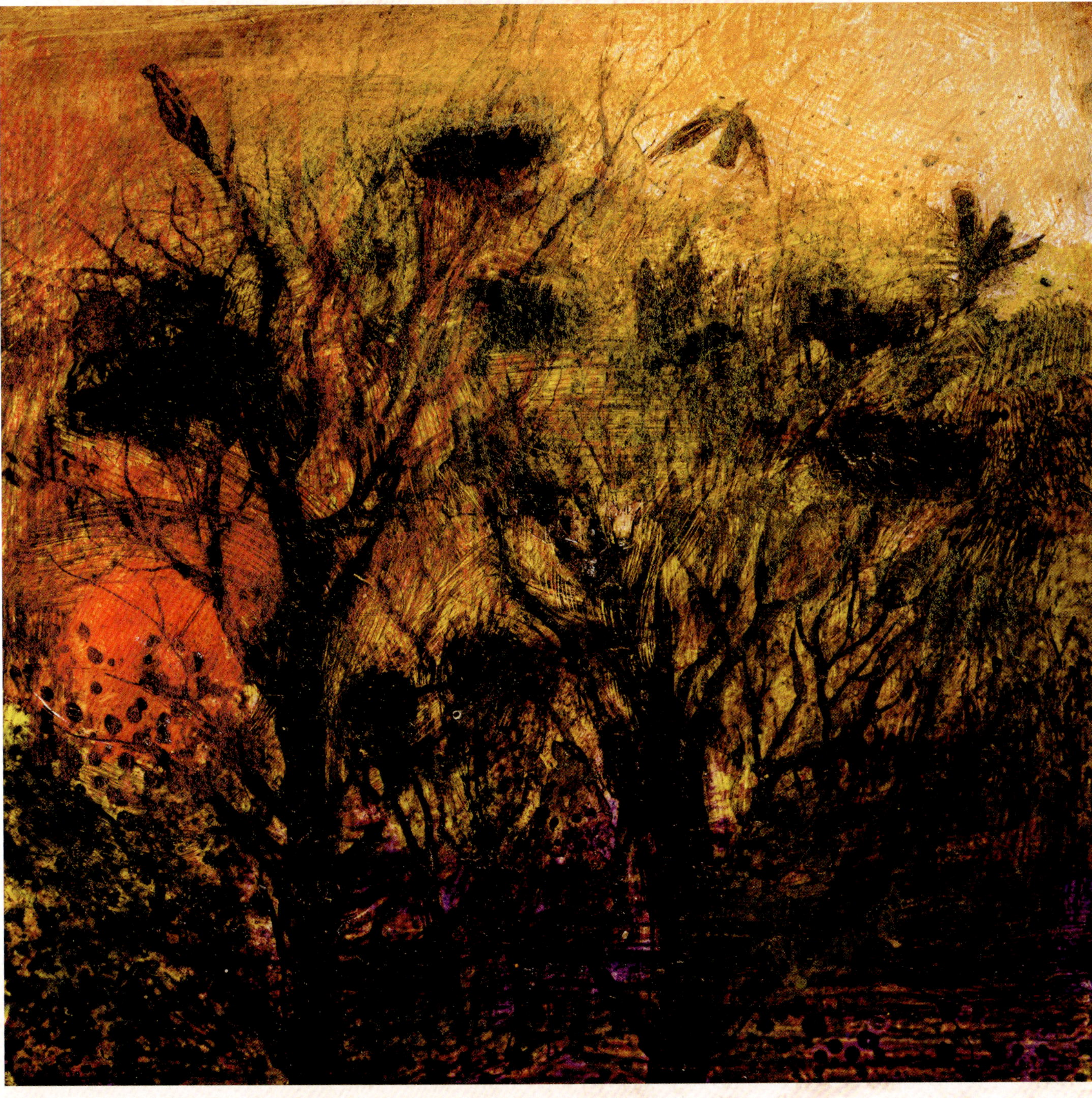

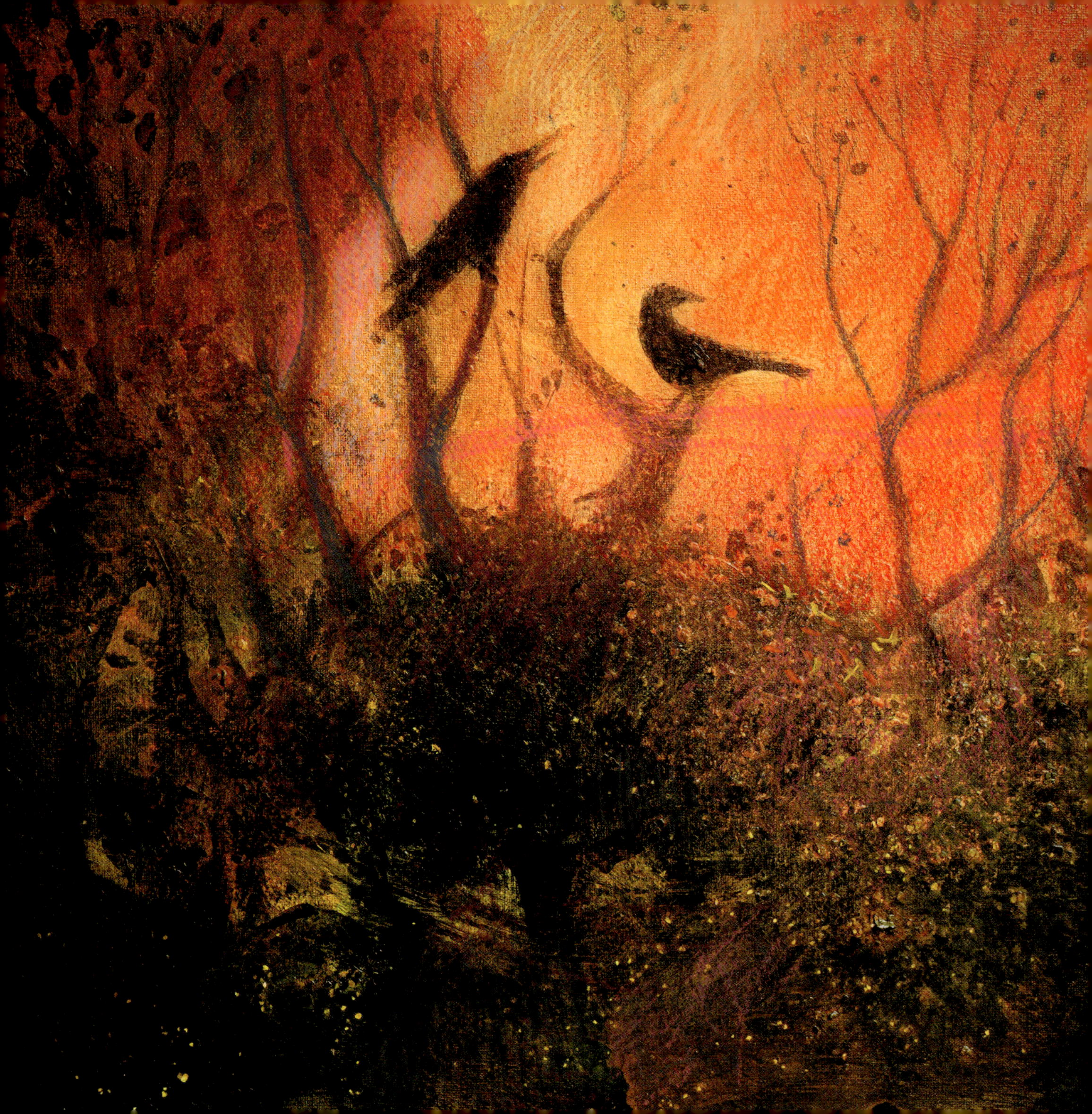

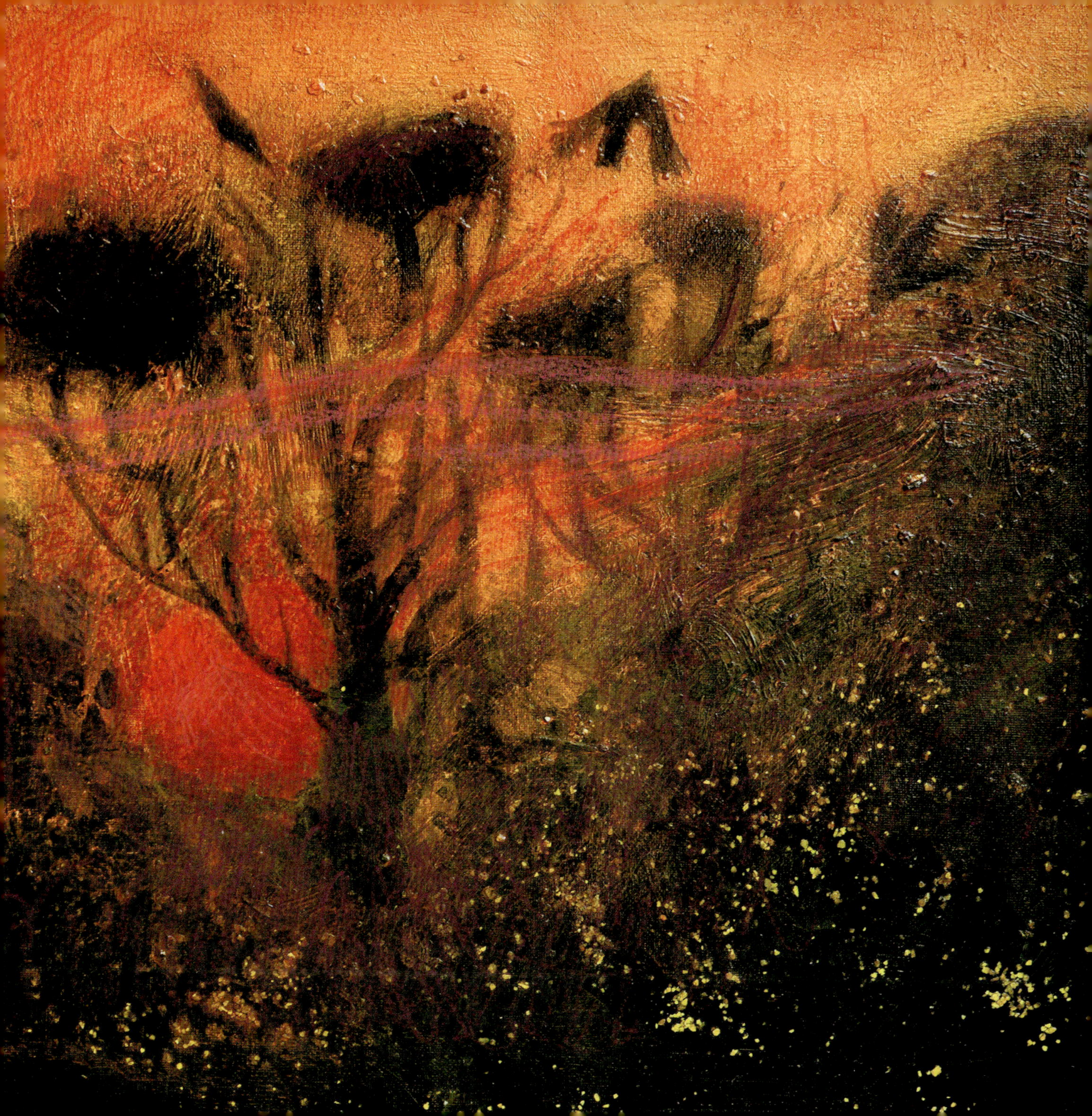

High up in ash trees
black rooks sway in twig dense nests,
calling rough questions,
as sun dances down
through the tangled trees,
flickering orange,
black,
apple crimson,
and plunges into the wood,

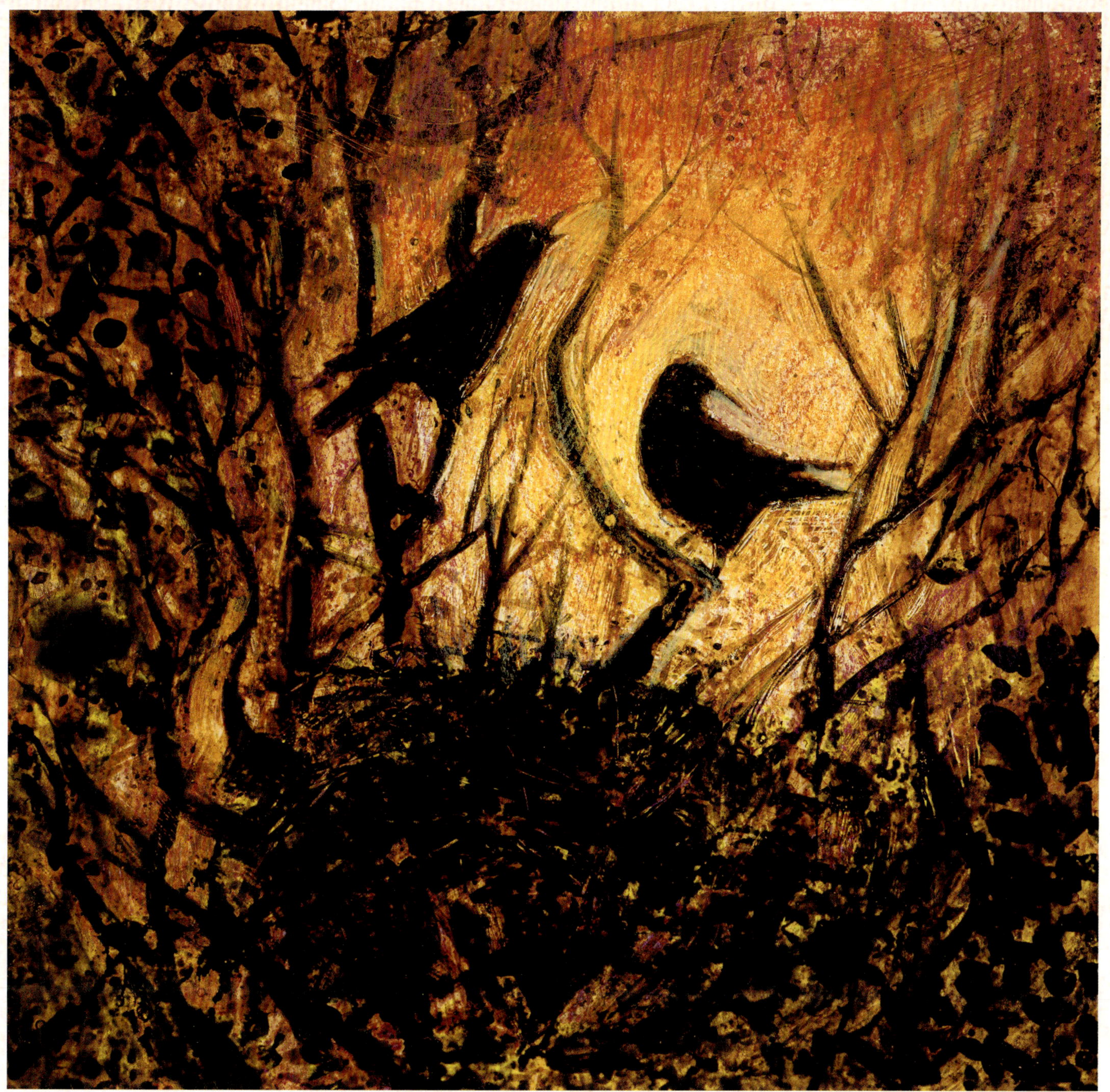

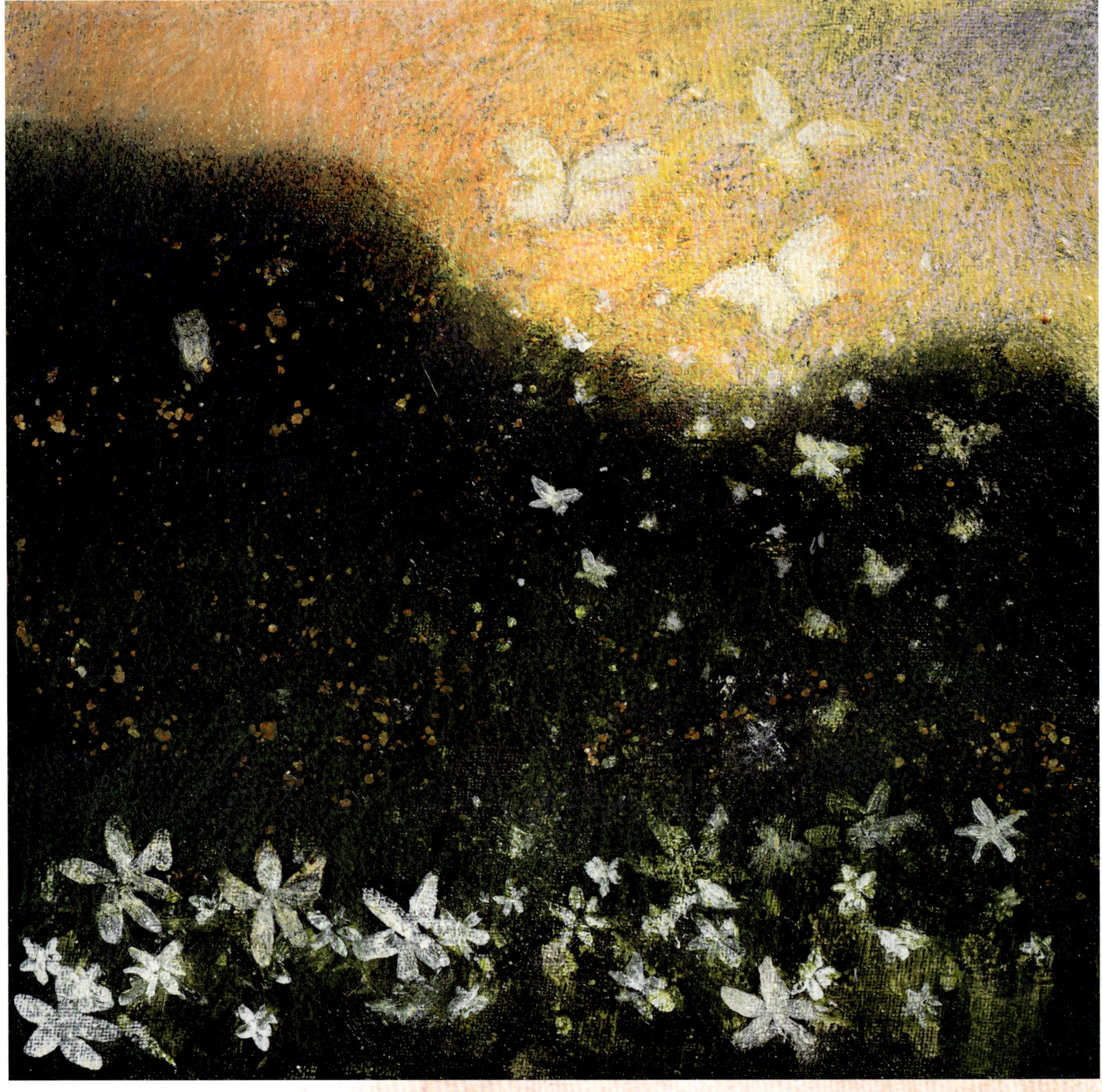

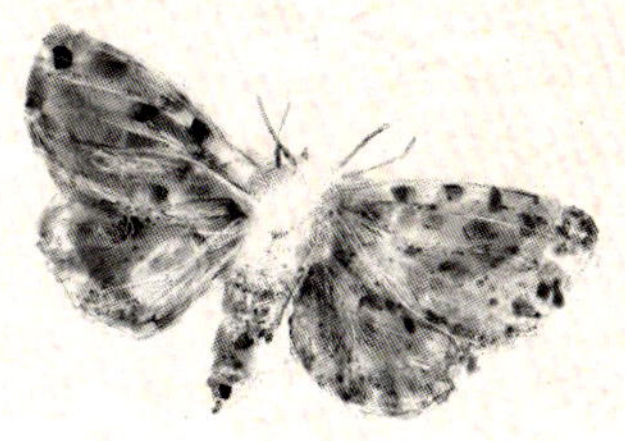

where moonflowers sleep,
where moths are
secret, white, soft,
fluttering
in the descending light.

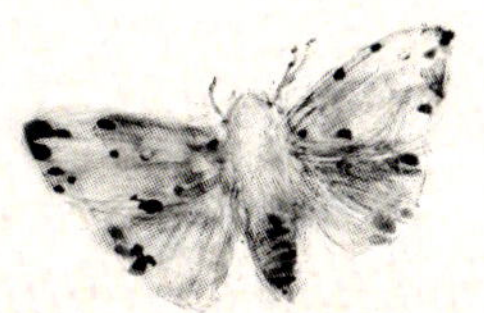

I sit
and I call twilight to me.

In the distance,
she answers
Kee witt
Kee witt

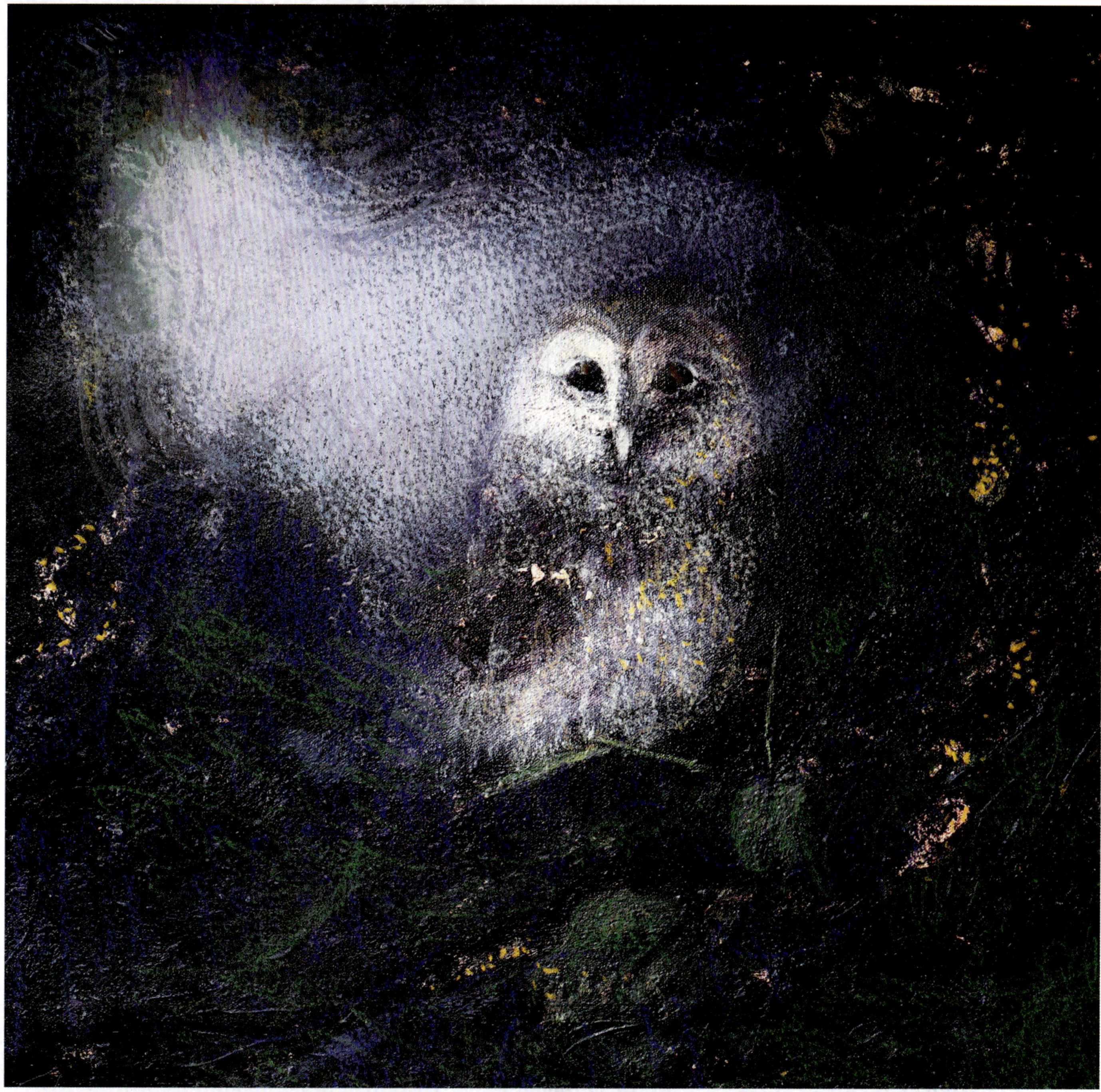

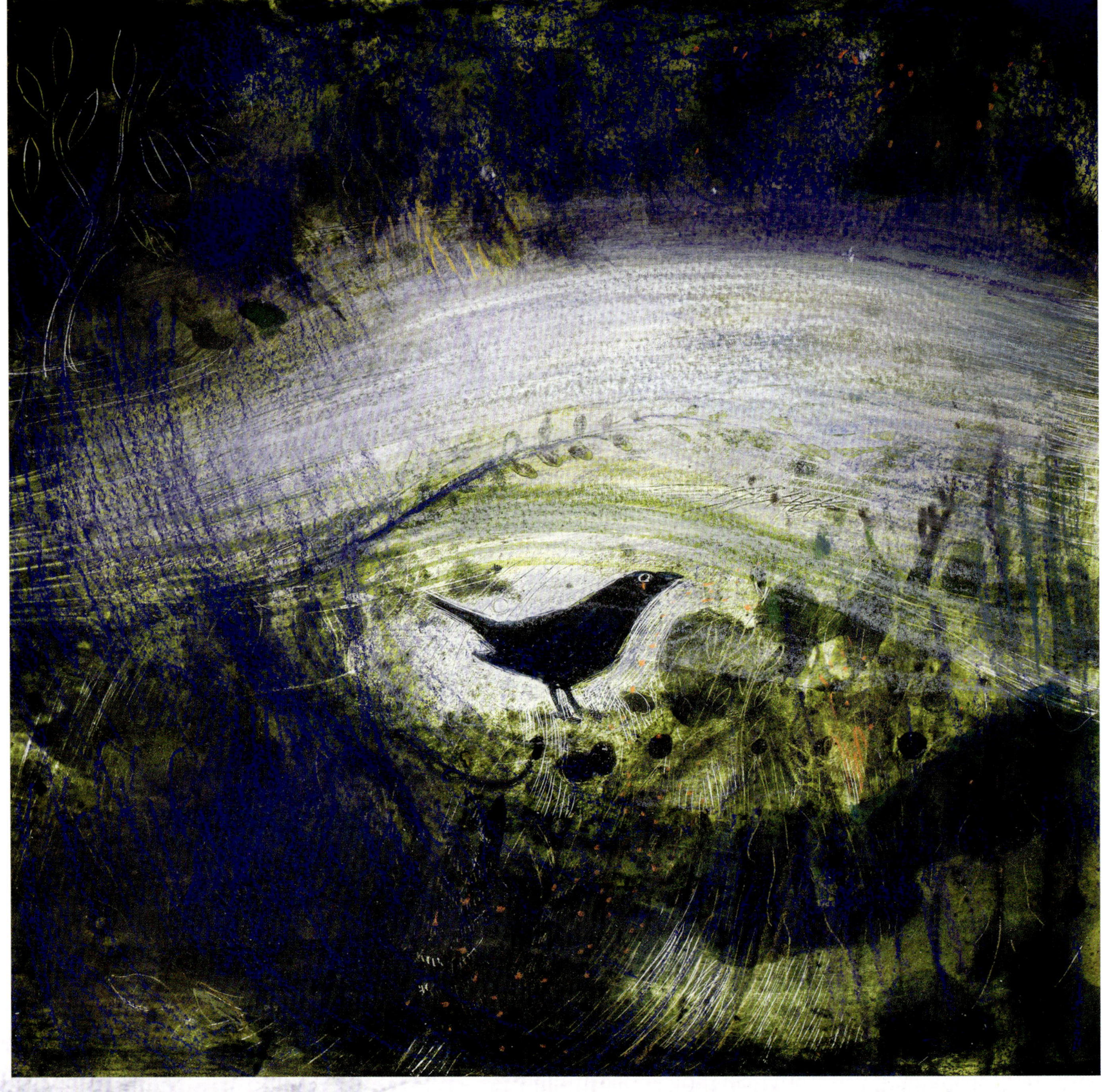

Evening's star glimmers in blackbird's eye
as I call darkling to me.

Closer,
she answers.

My feathered fingers creep
through grass and bracken,
filling the holes of mouse and vole
with tawny shadows,
remembering where snake likes to go
and hedgehog burrows.

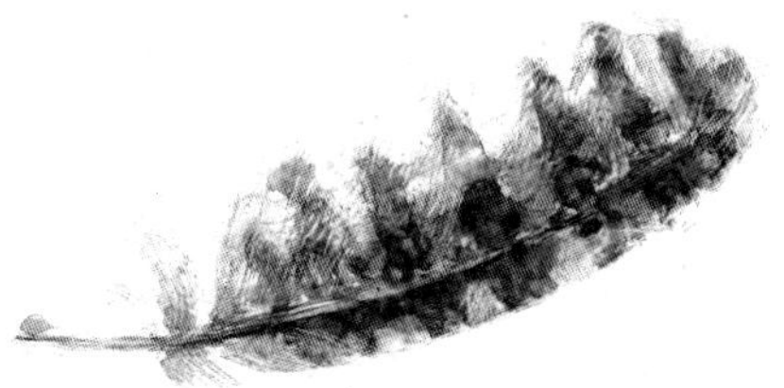

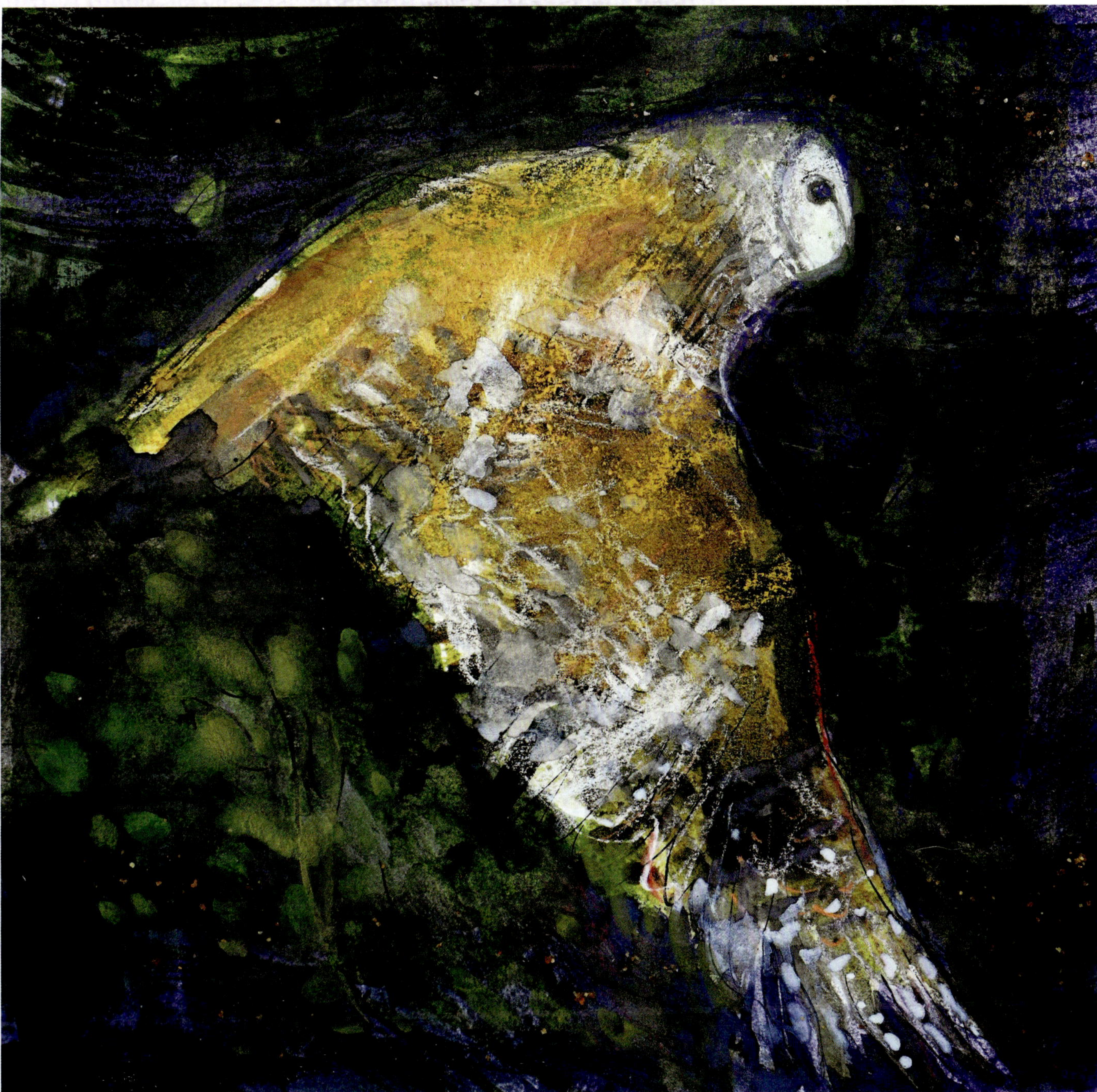

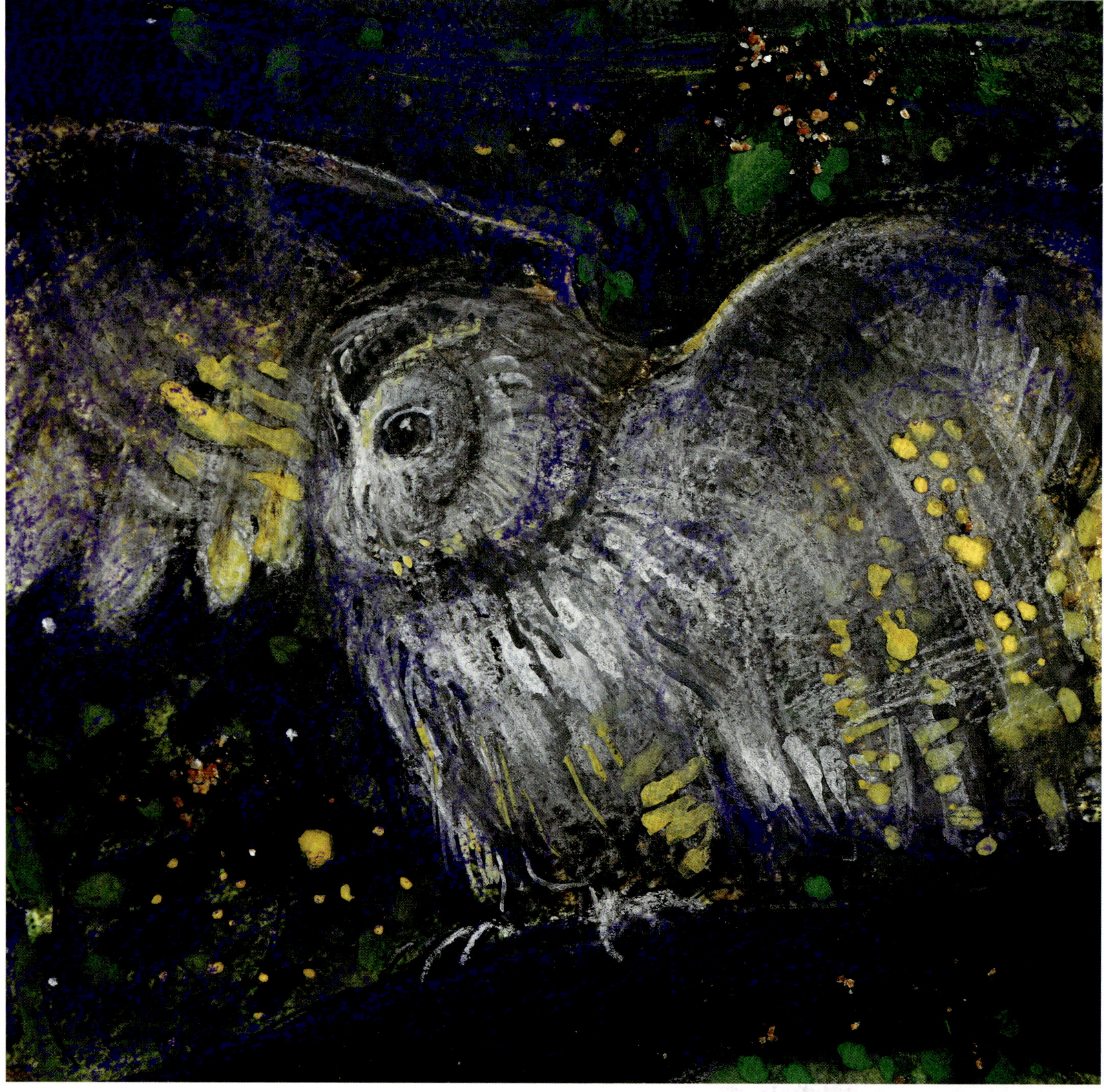

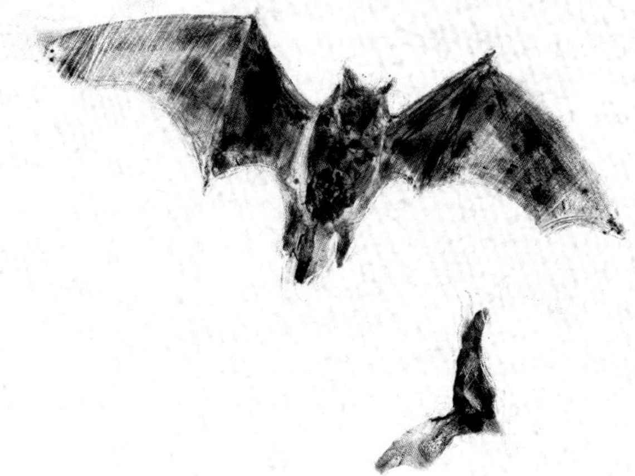

I sit and I listen
to night's secrets
sliding between branches,
stealing under ferns,
cloaking the wood with the velvet of bats,
a soft whirr of wings

and I watch
as planets brighten

I call
and constellations
prickle,
twinkling
into the arms of great trees,
diamond patterning woodland blackness.
Hoooo hoooo hoooo
Nearby,
she answers
Kee witt
Kee witt

I sit
smelling stars,
older than the trees,
as old as night,
as old as I am.

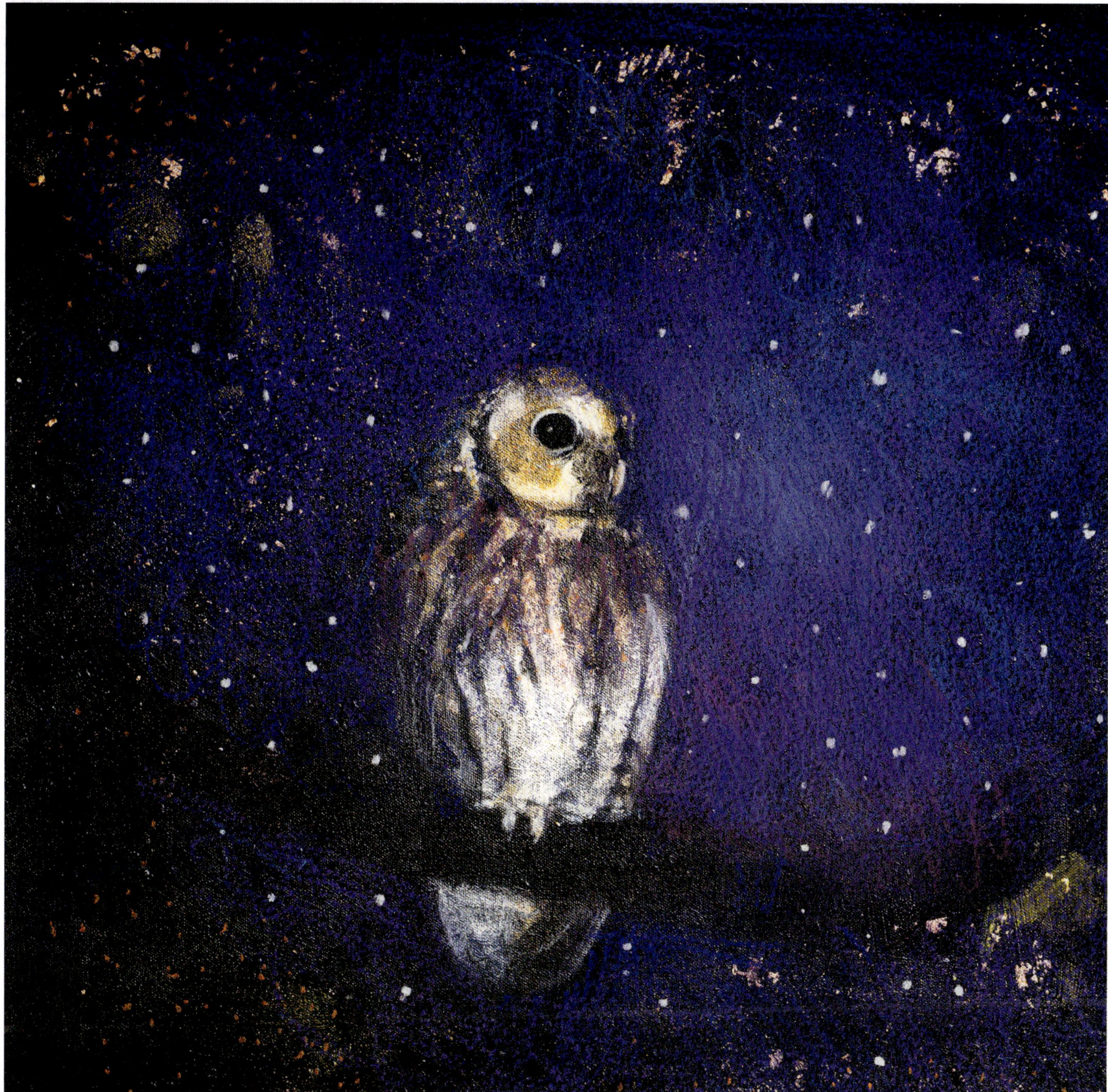

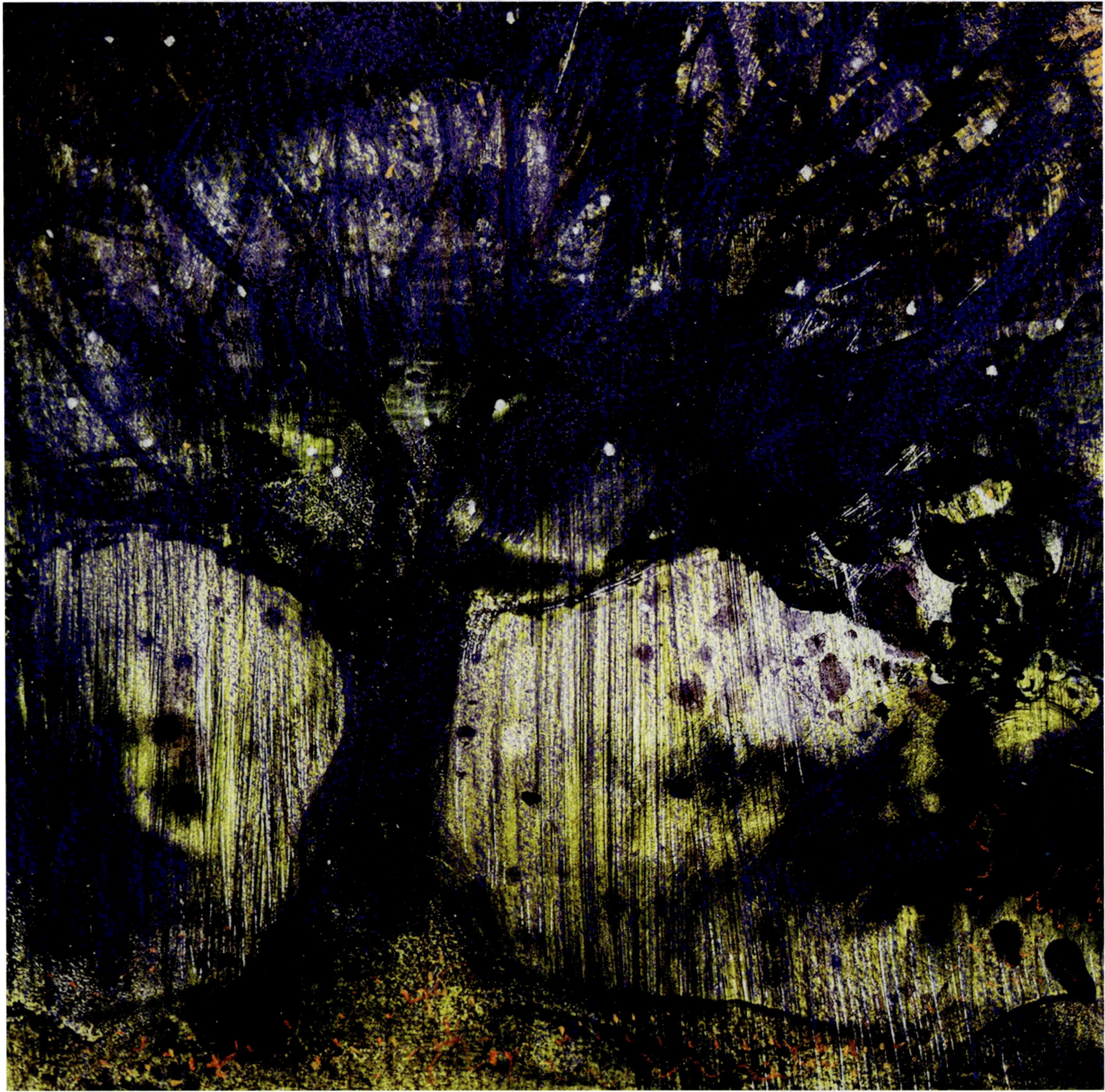

Stillness has fallen,
sound shrunk to
creaks of branches rubbing,
the squeak and scratching of trees talking.
A shimmer of leaf fall,
scuttering.
Twigs shifting
as squirrel runs chittering by.

I sit
and I call,

I sit
and I listen.

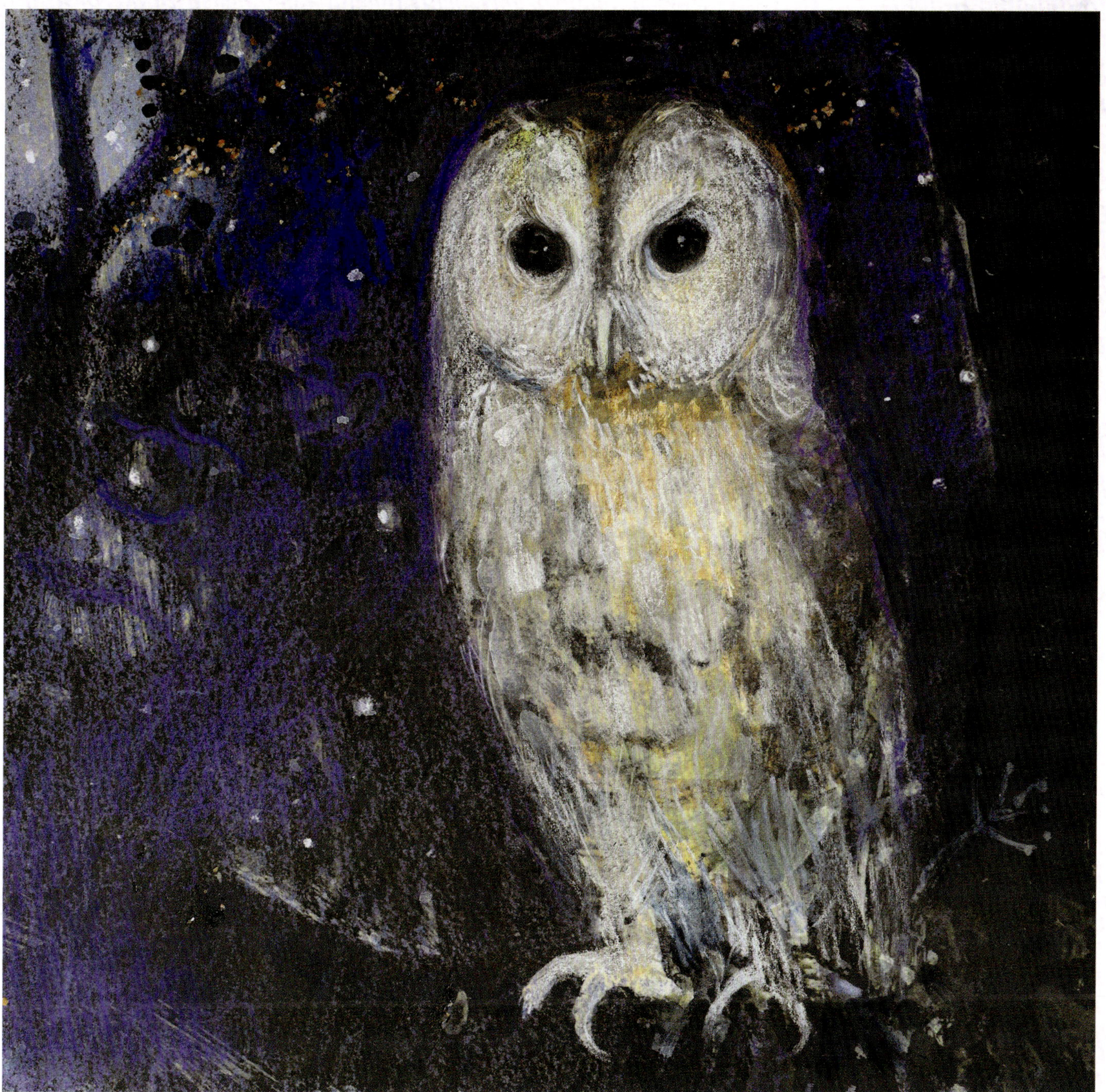

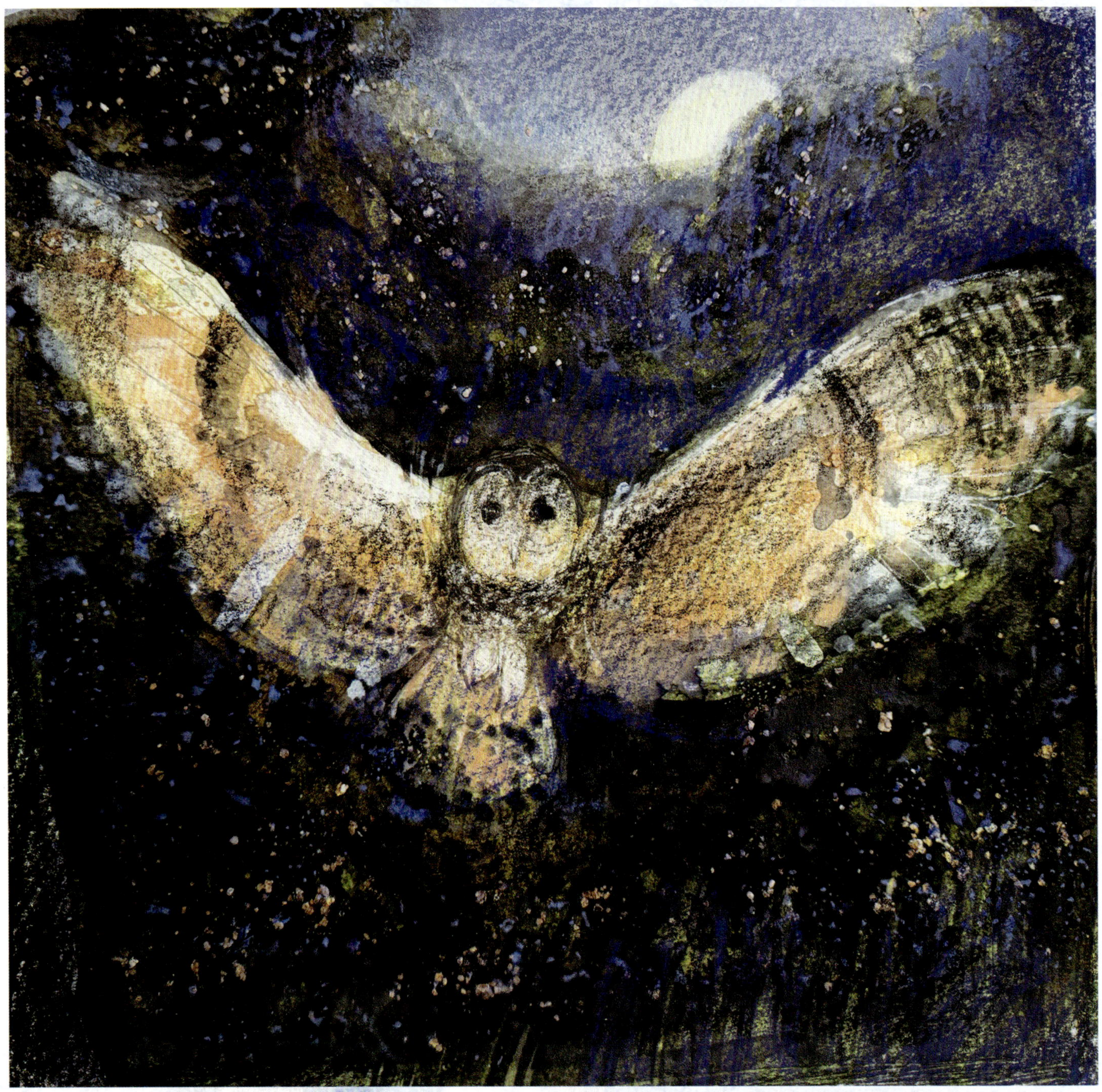

Slowly, slowly
the owl moon, the hunter's moon,
cornfield gold
rises
booming
into night's nectar,
casting a spell
entrancing moths,
gilding bats.

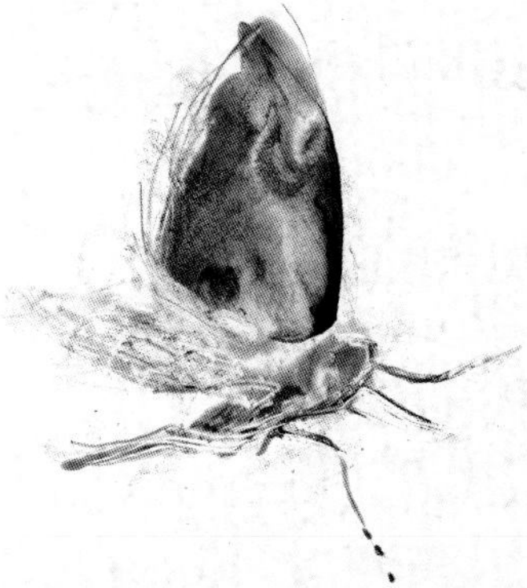

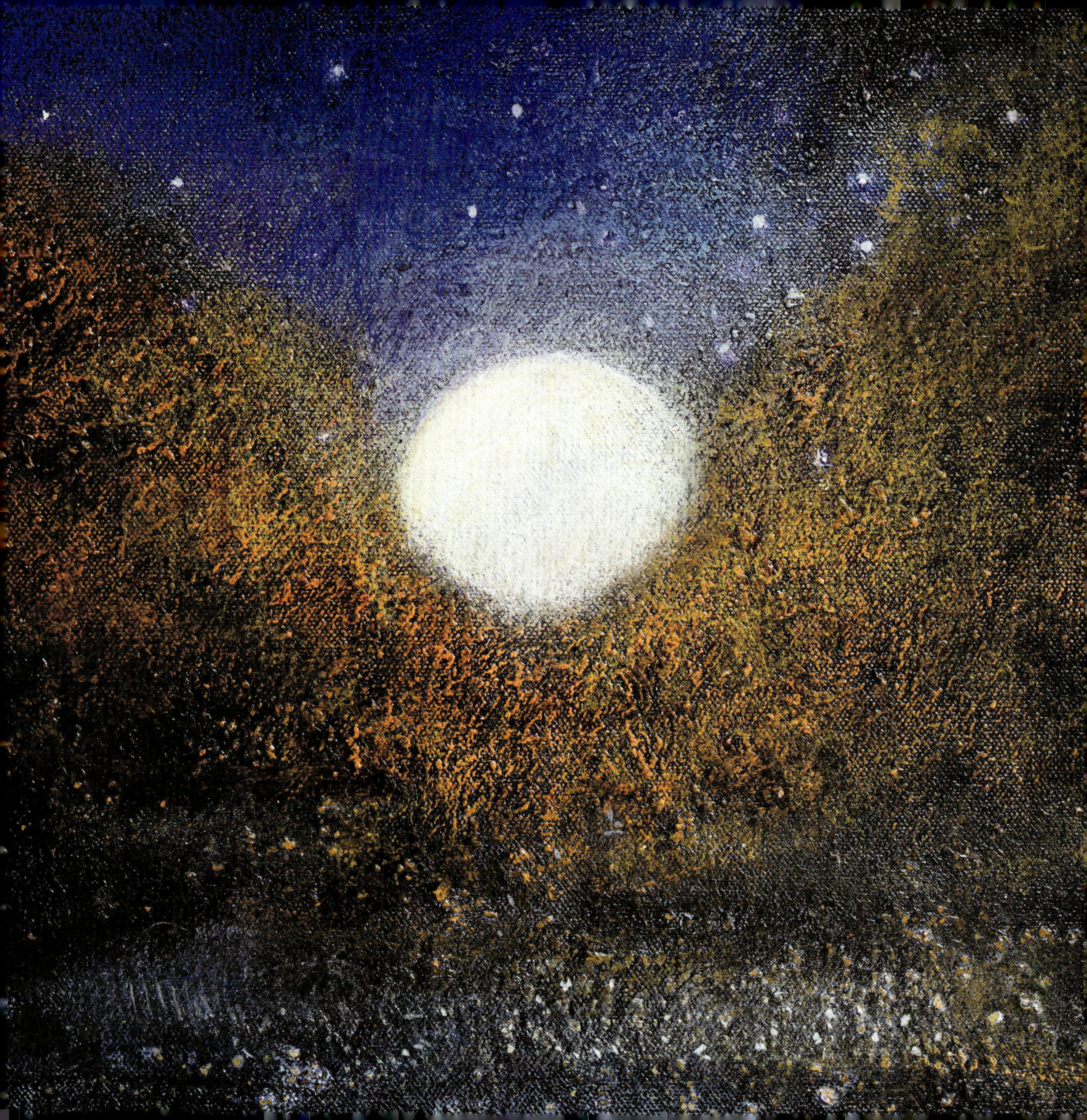

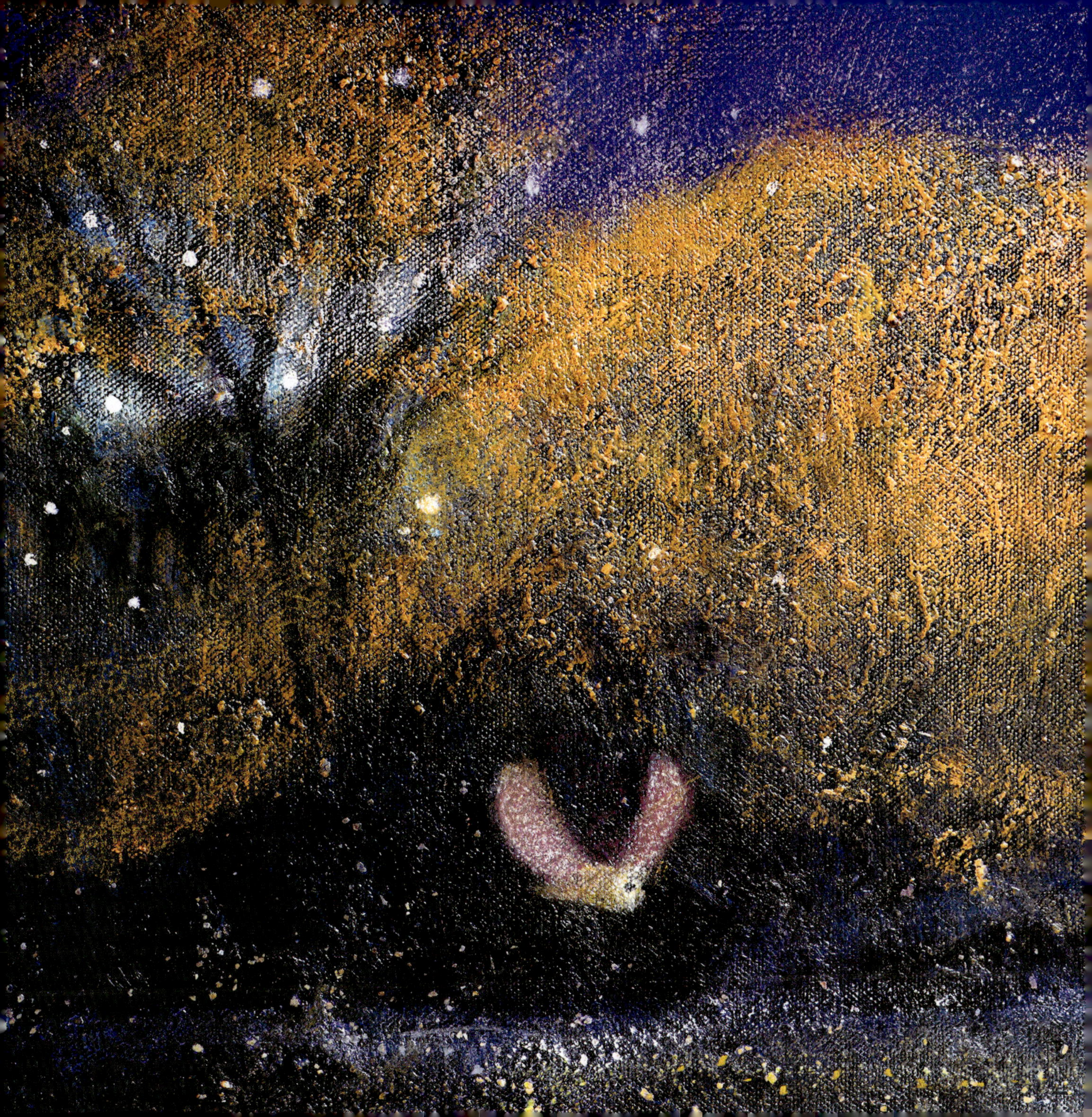

I am oak
I am leaf
I am star
I am moon
I am time
I am past
I am present
I am hungry.
This is my land,
the Darkling Wood.

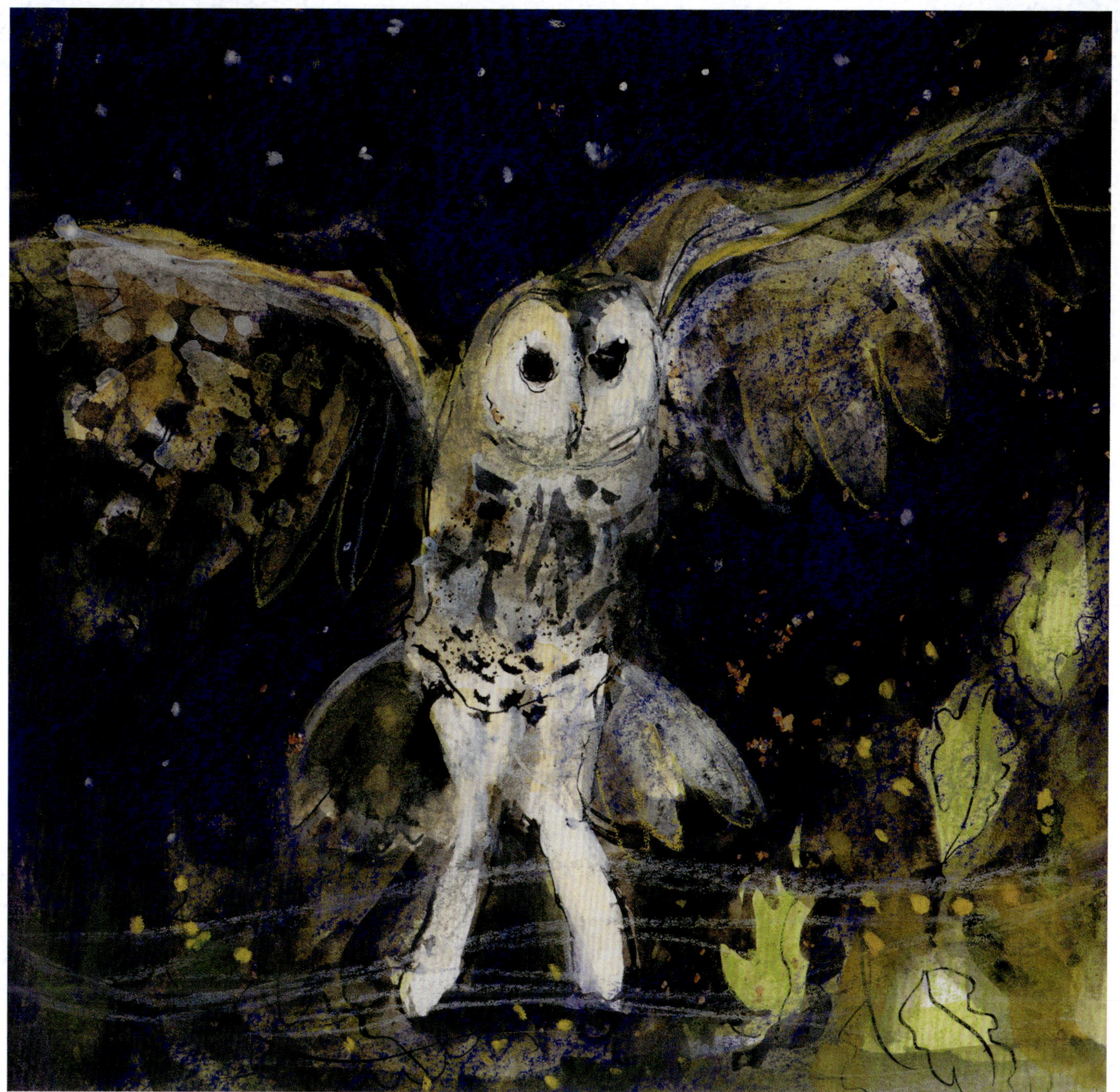

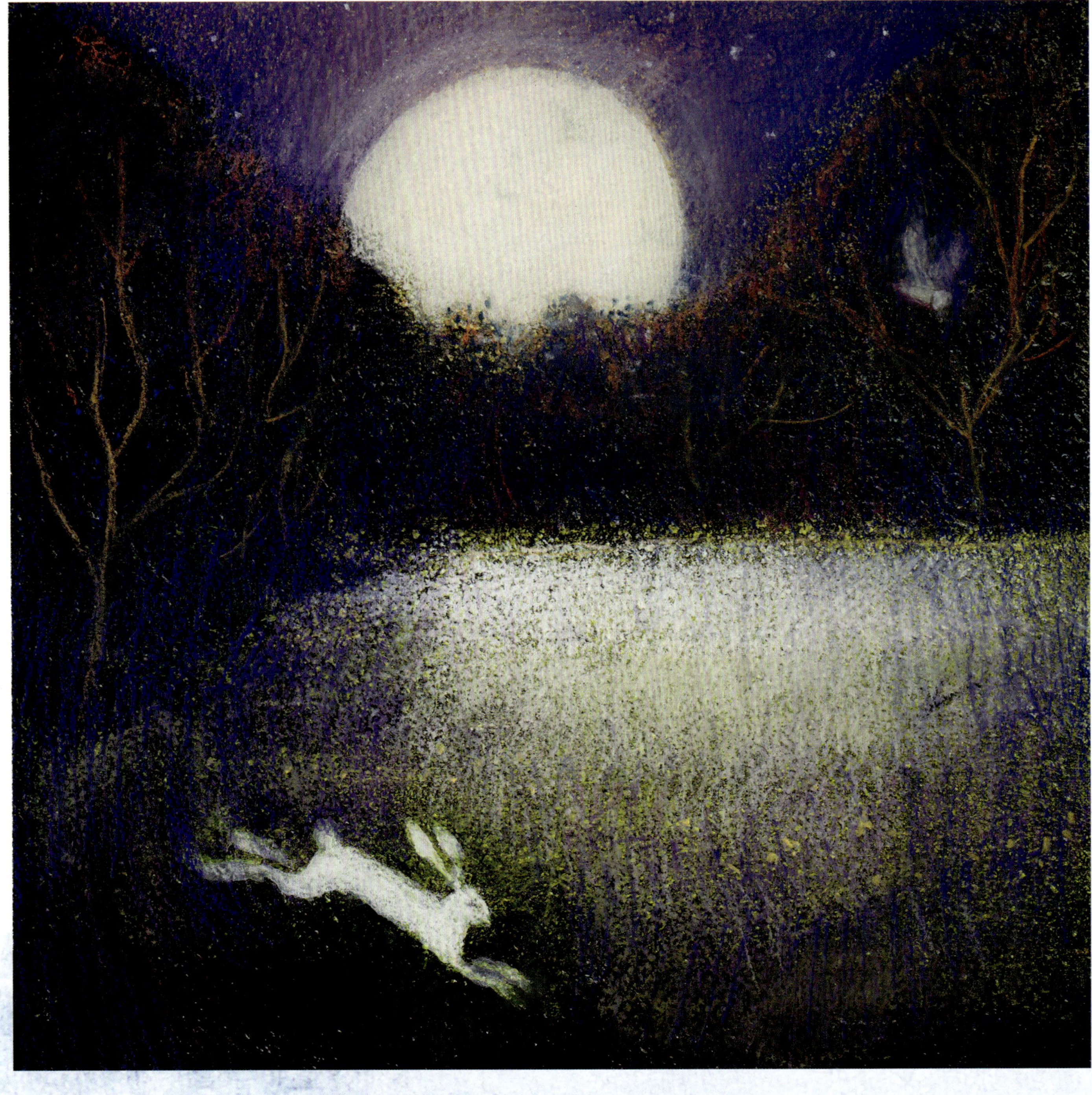

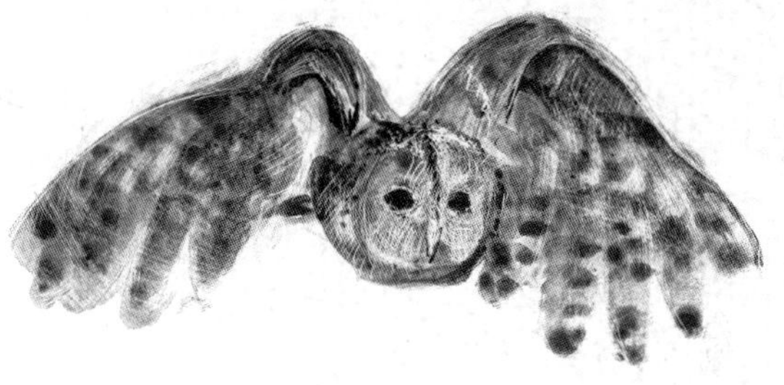

I sweep
silent
along the sooty hedgerow,
where dormouse lives and wren nests.
Past fields where rabbits run and fox slinks

I drift
between
giant hawthorn,
whose confetti petals, bridal white,
melt into air’s green perfume
where swift and swallow dive
with bees
and cuckoo calls,
mocking,
all day long.

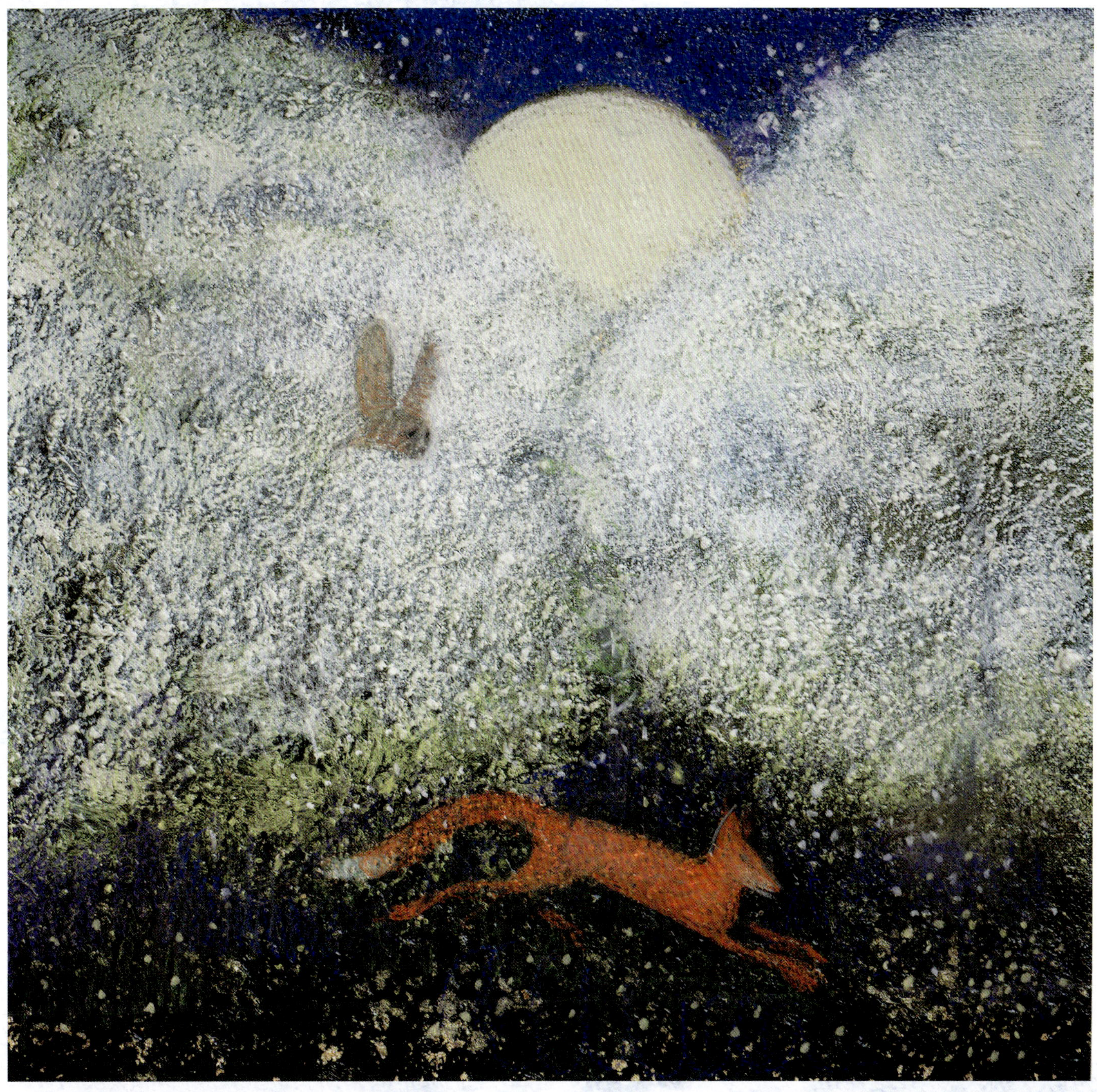

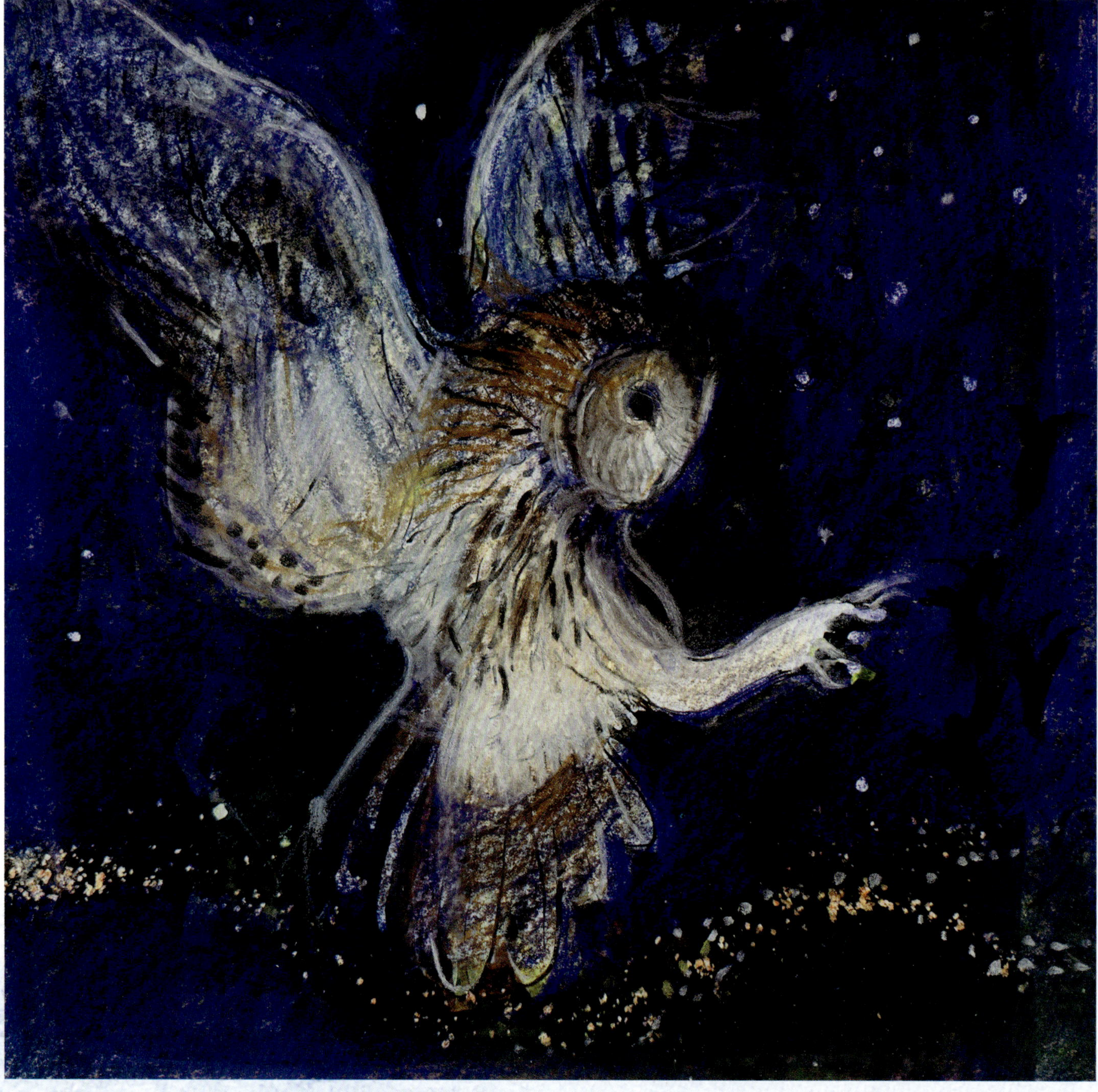

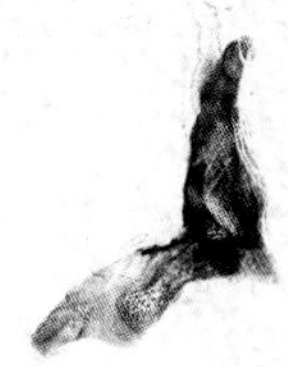

I float
up
over the heavy yew,
damp air alive,
winged,
blurring,
breathing bats,
I snap,
feasting.

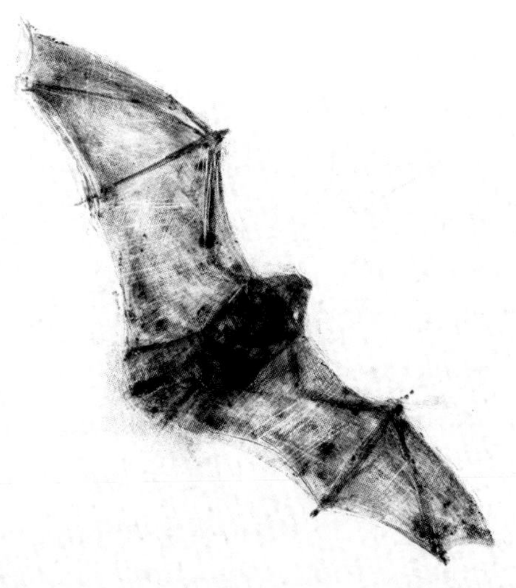

I glide
by ancient wayfaring tree,
where nightingale sings of love,
weaving silver threads to moon
and back,
an echoing chain,
shimmering with stars and fireflies.

I call night to me

in the distance,
she answers.

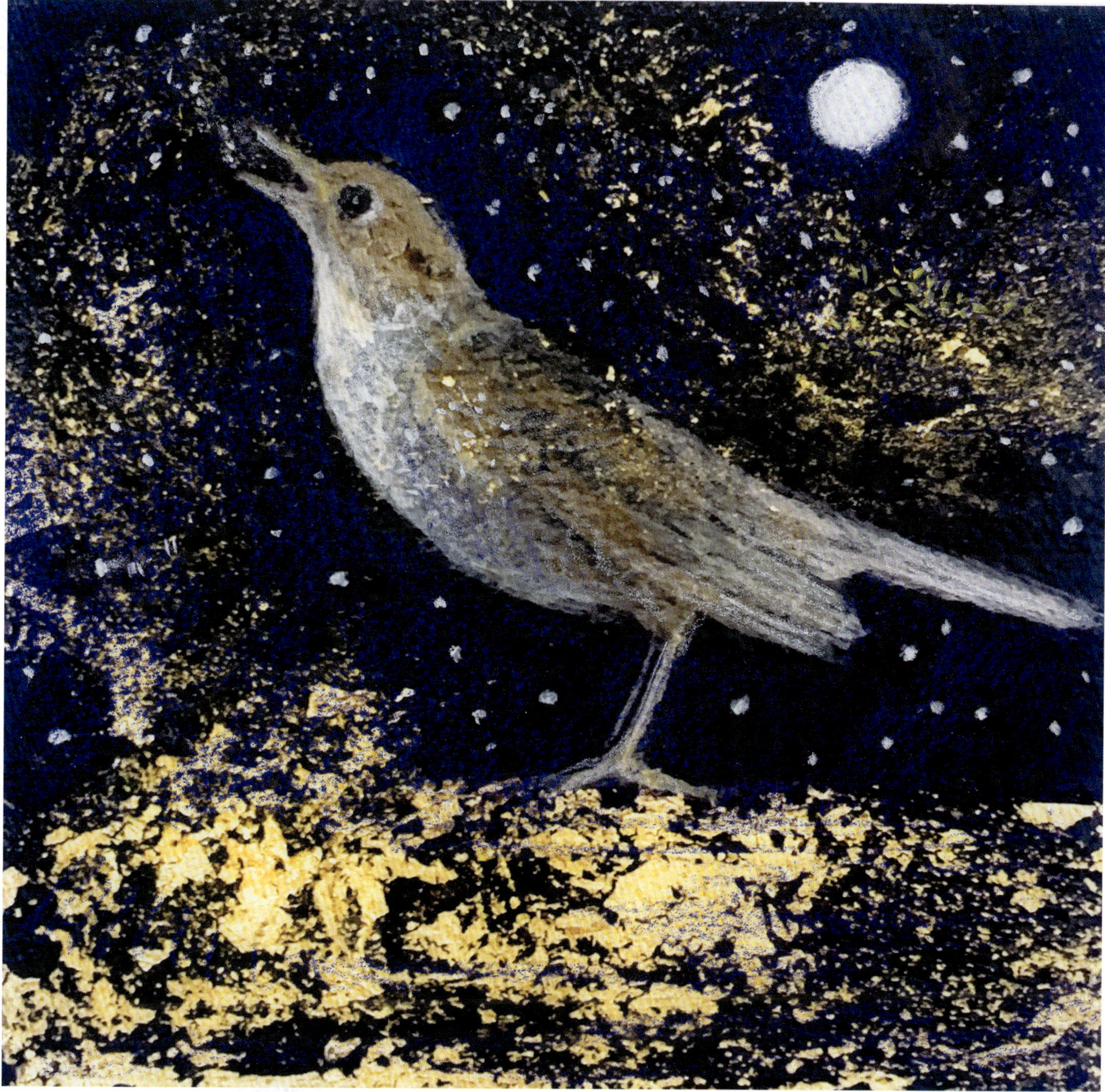

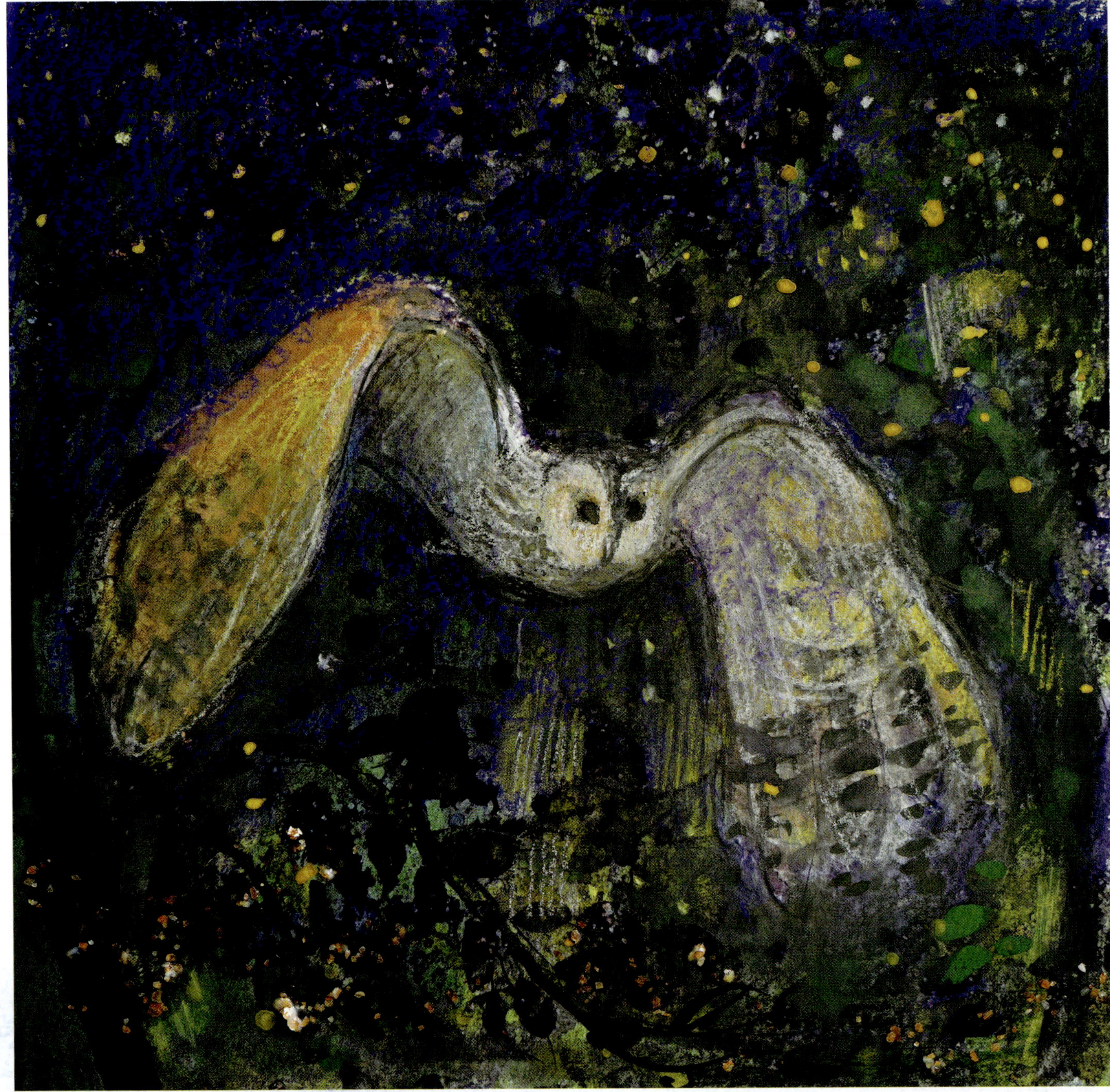

I fly
through hazel copses

I circle
around forest's king
mighty oak,

who, year on year, spreads his pollen on the wind,
cradles birds and small creatures,
teeming bugs and spiders,
dancing butterflies.

Sheds golden leaves and acorns to
vole and mouse
scurrying through silty richness.

Sends his messages rooting deep down
under the listening earth

I drop
past whistling holly trees,
druid dark, crowned with red berries

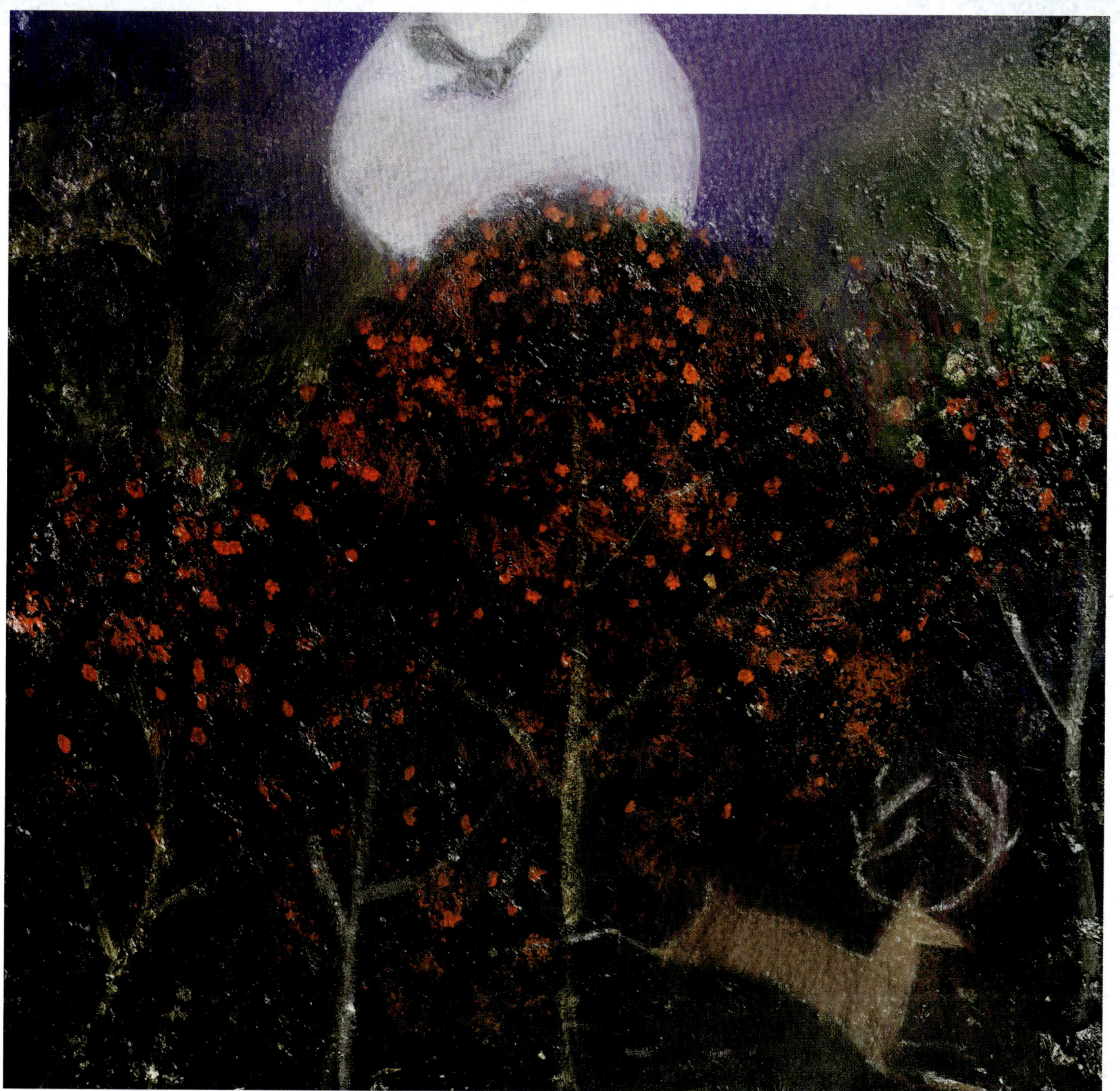

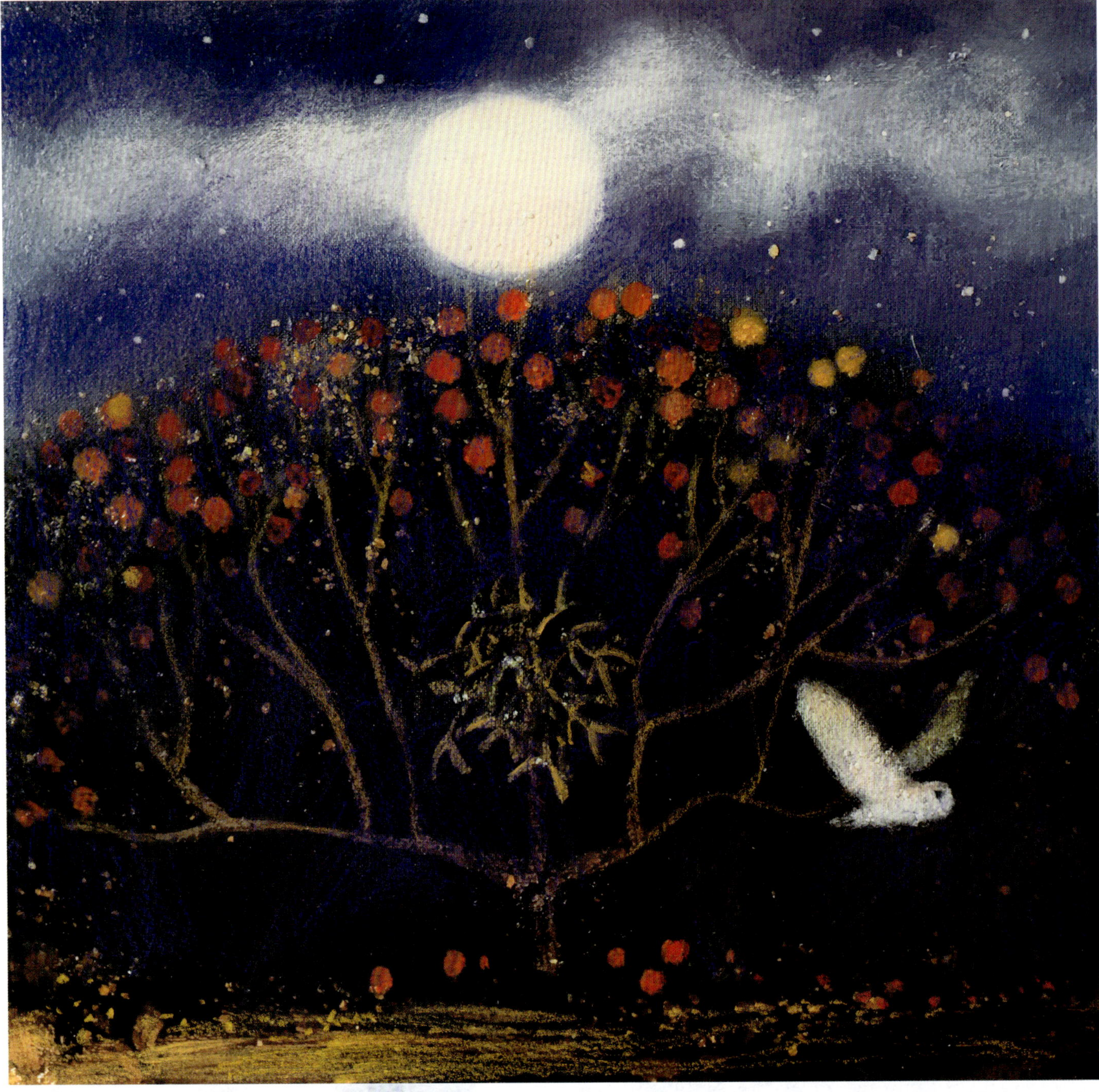

I turn
to the old orchard
where she hunts:
a ghost glimmering
sweet heart of the moon.
Swooping between trees,
a beating clock of claw and feather,
hush winged, in half light.
She screams
shattering night.

I fly on from tree to tree
call darkling to me.

In the distance,
she answers

Kee witt
Kee witt

beech,
silent yew,
dark holly,
slender elm,
rowan,
hazel,
hawthorn, berry red,
graceful birch,
ash,
oak.

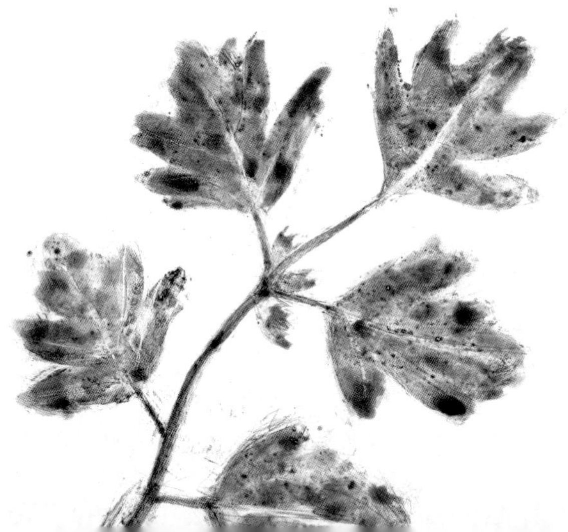

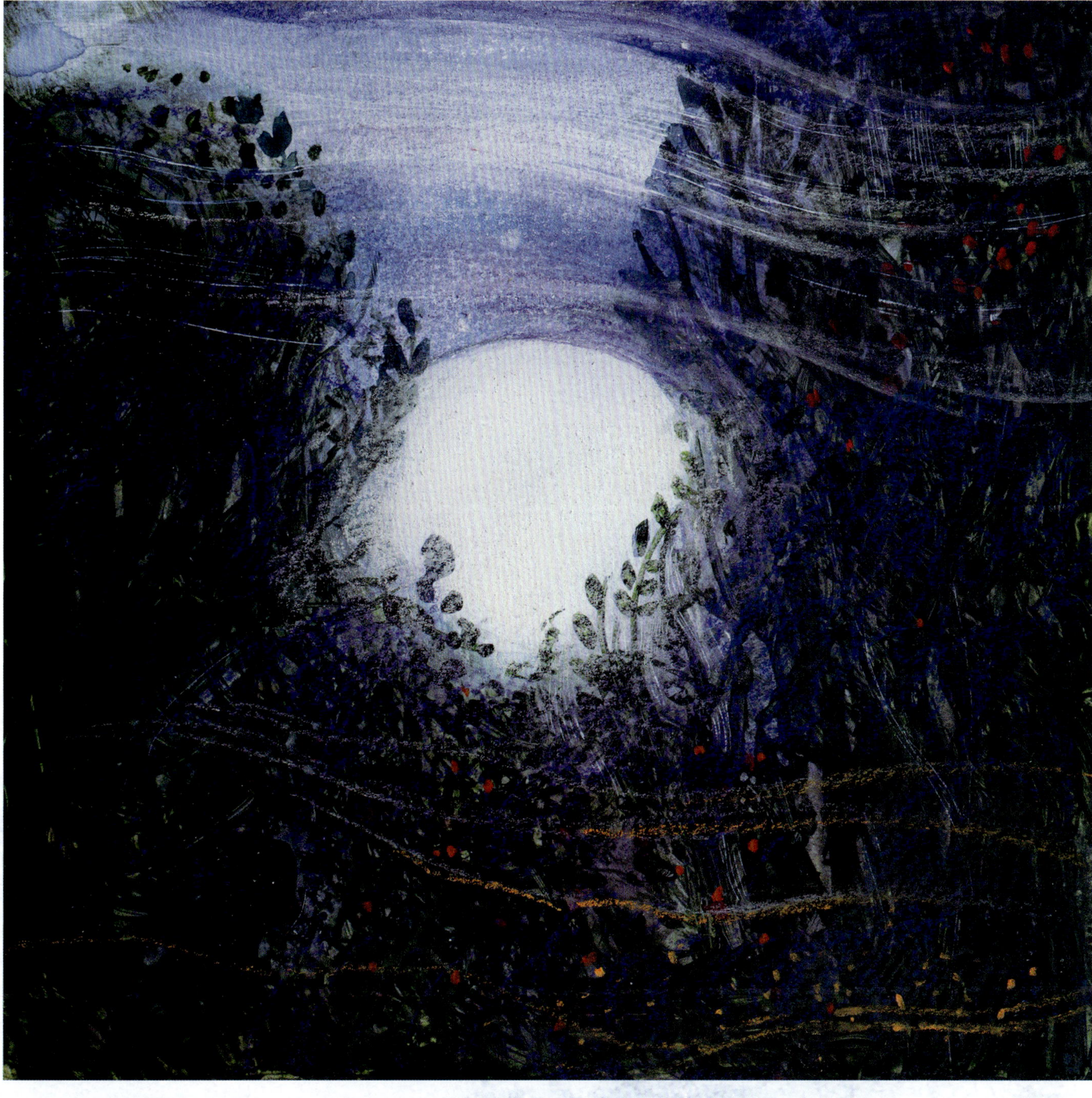

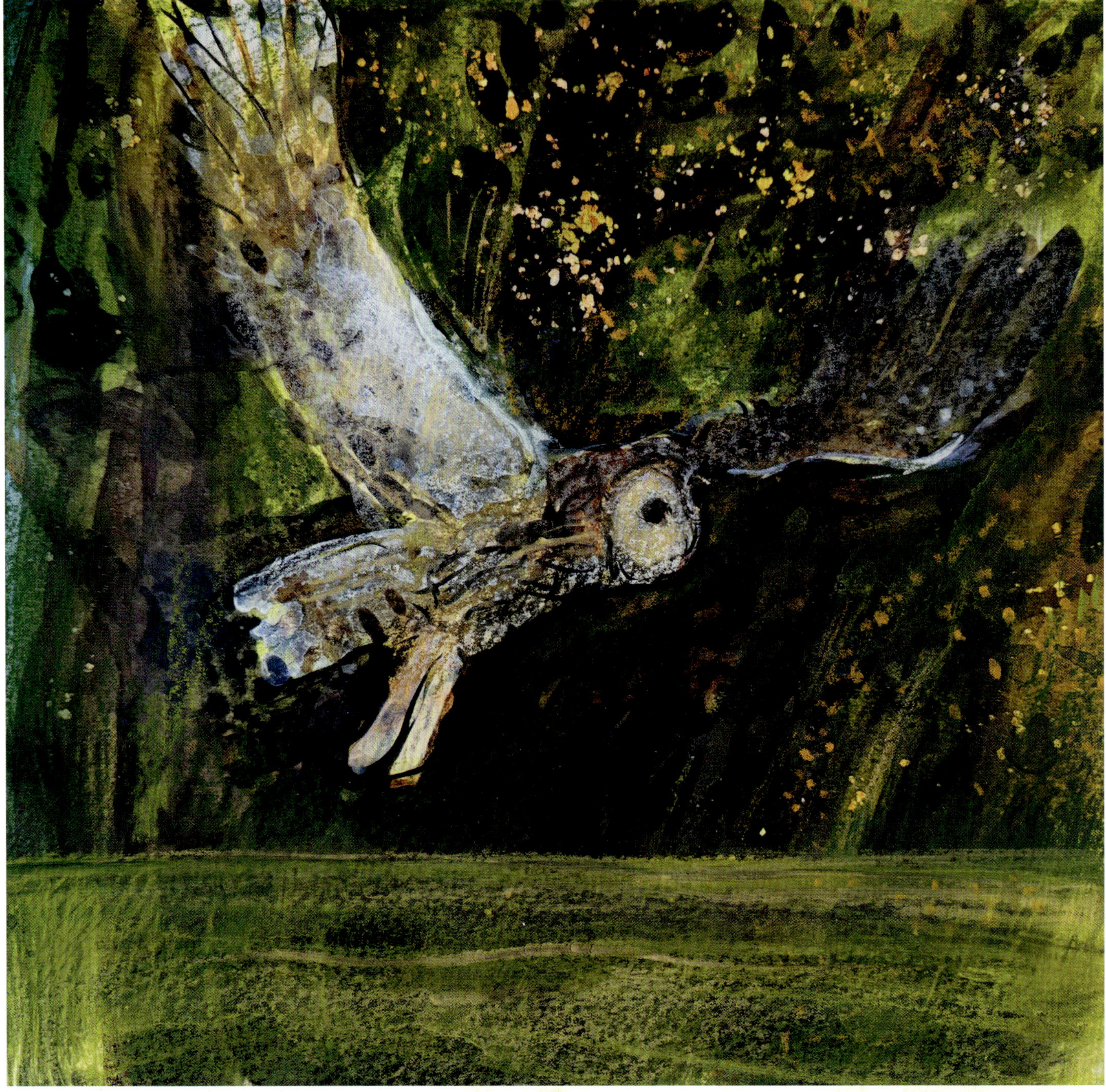

Listen.
I am Old Brown.
I am Darkling.

I fly,
beating wings along
the running river
pulling, swirling,
always rushing, never listening,
laughing, glistering,
frothing, splashing.
Cutting rock,
smoothing
stones,
loosening soil,
polishing root and branch,
transporting feathers, leaves,
corpses.

I call
Hooo hoooo hoooooo

In deep eddies,
beneath lands levels,
cool-bellied trout hover,
heads against the flow

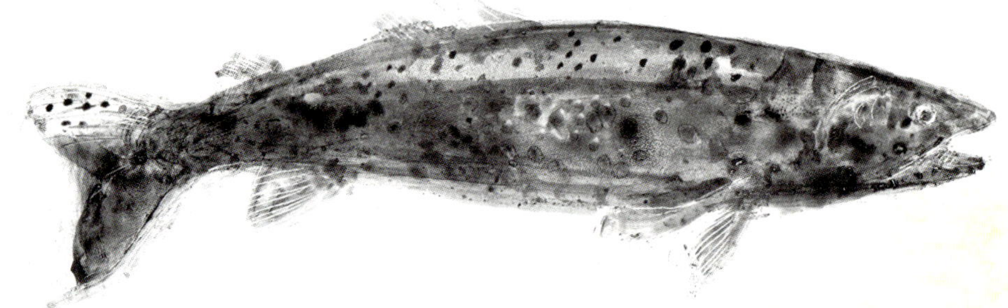

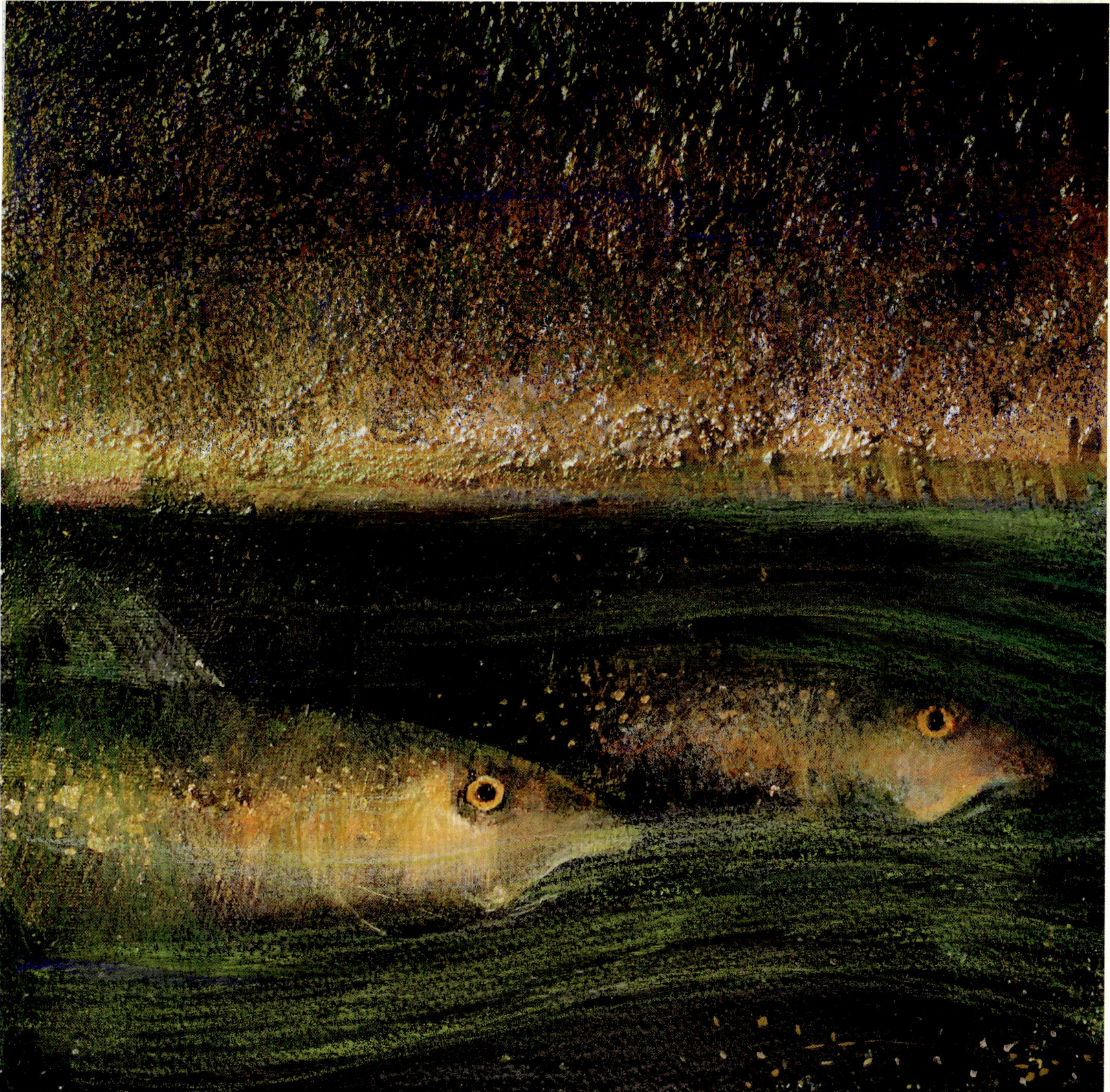

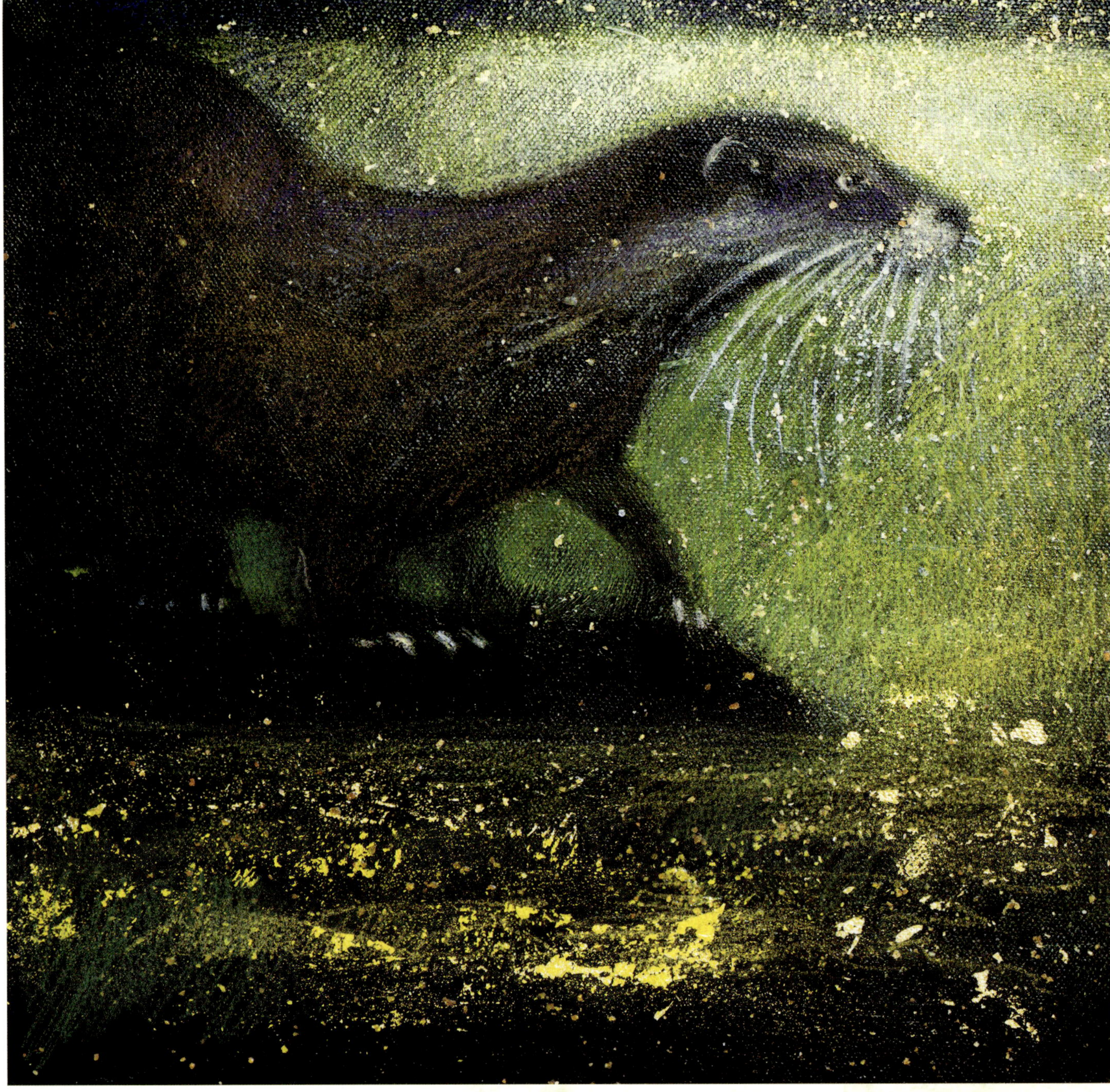

otter dives
a river pirate,
teeth gleaming,
whiskers shining.
Quicksilver,
a silver wick,
an oily slick,
bubbles splitting,
claws hitting,
tail flashing,
fish scatter
scramming in a flicker.

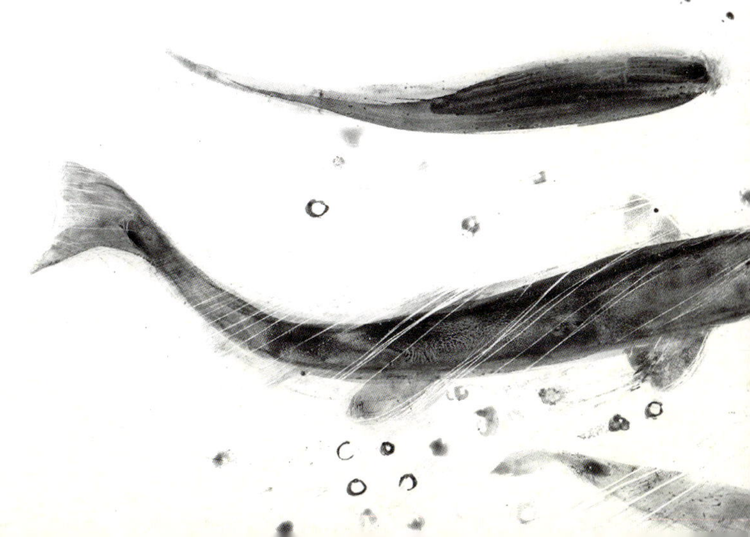

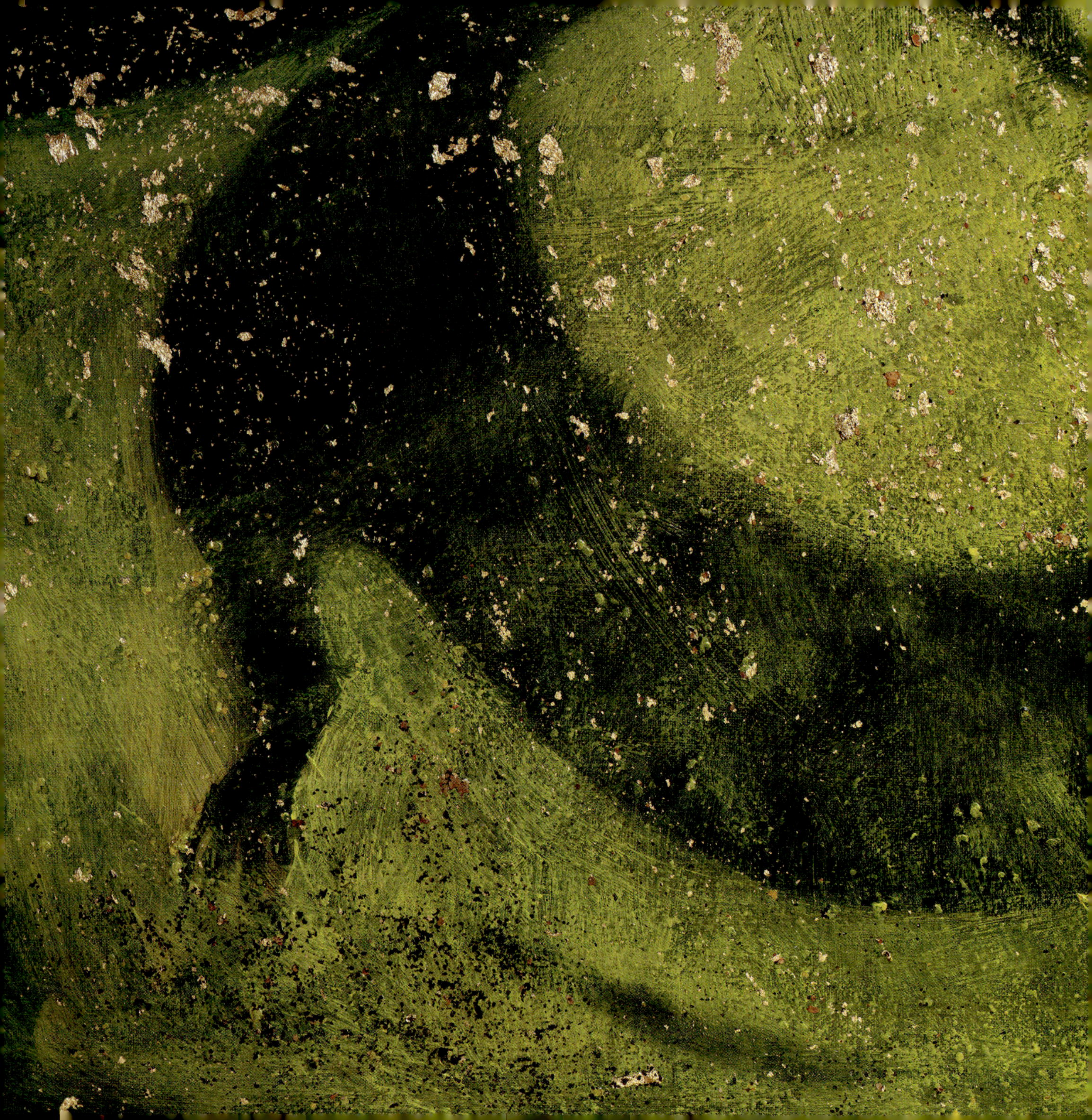

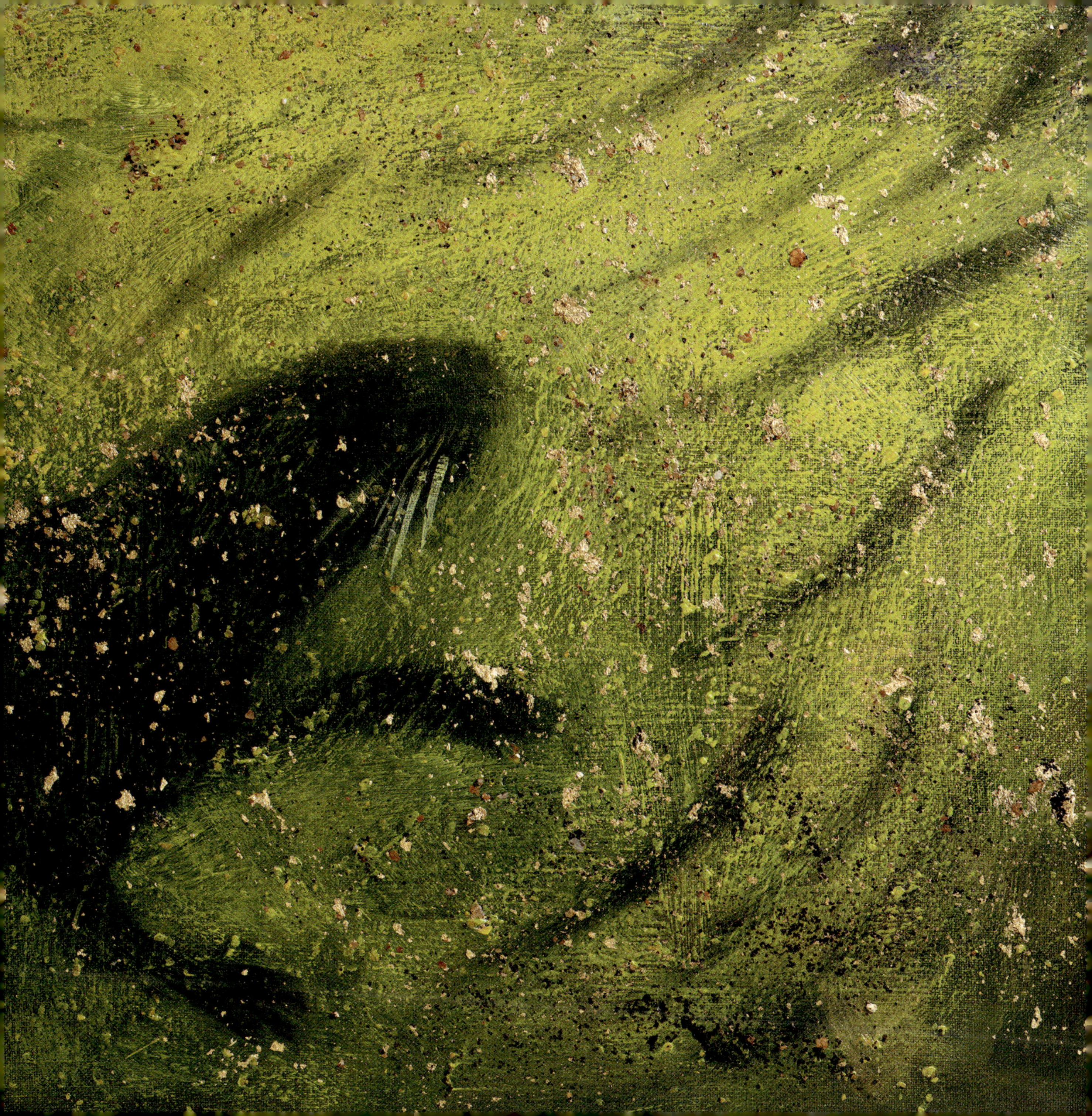

I fly
along the marshy plain
past heron,
who hunches stone still
in moonlight.

Waiting.

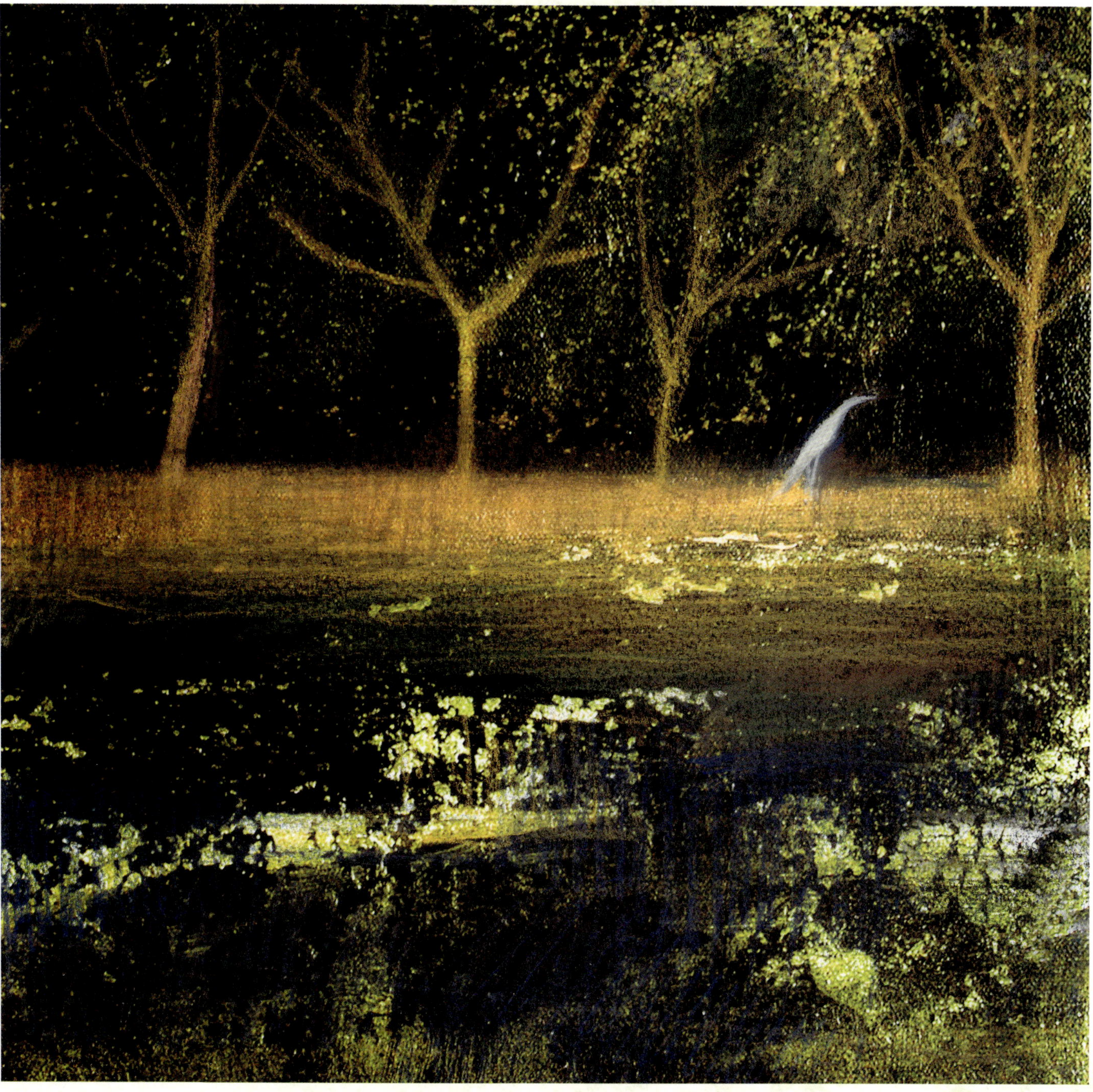

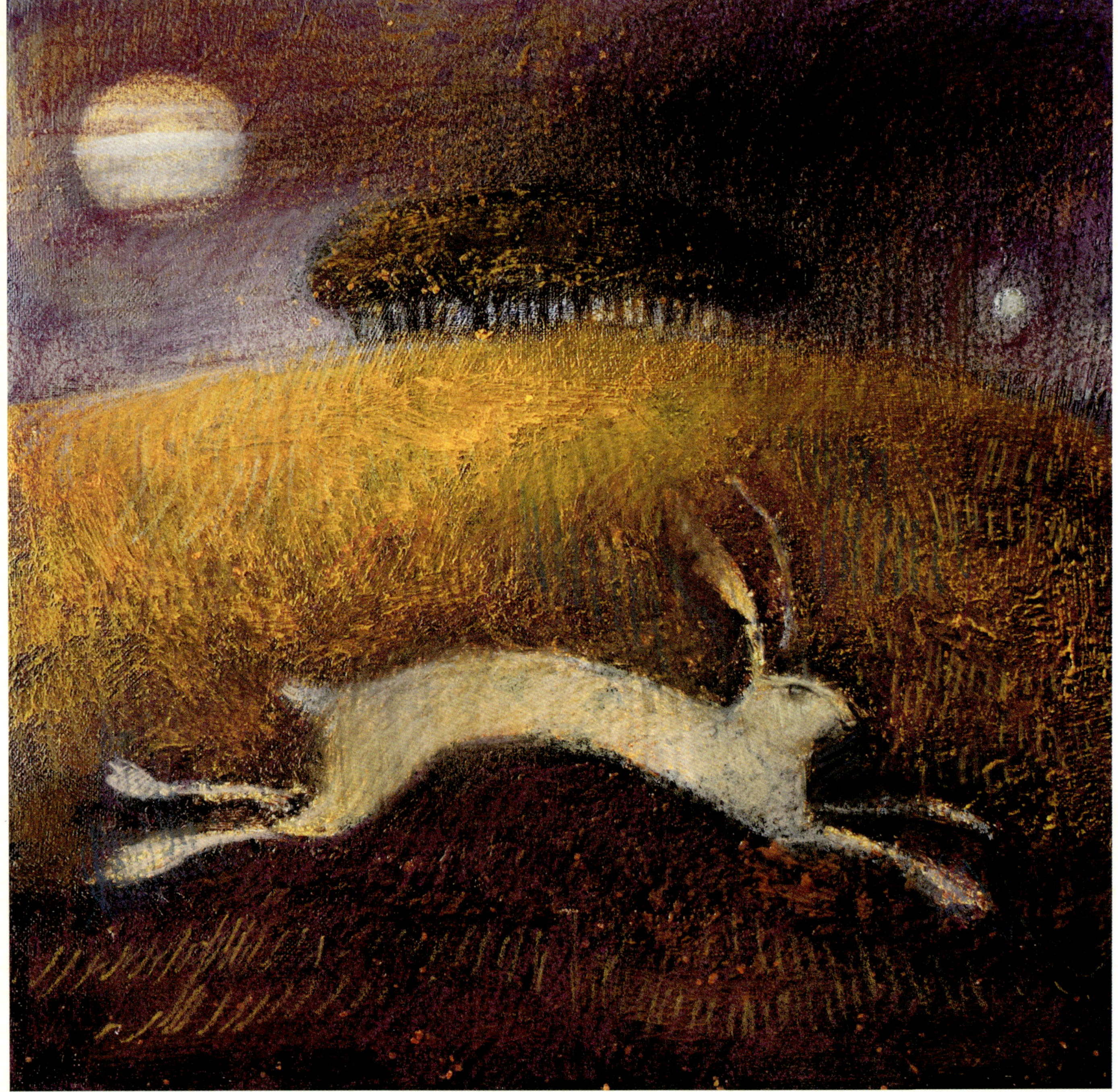

I fly
low
in fox dark
across stubbled cornfields
where hare,
neither earth nor air,
runs,
playing with shadows

I fly up
to lonely copse at hill top,
river song rises
as wind lifts.

Moon dances,
loose
among scudding clouds
I feel
a squall blow in,
sheeting rain
gusting,
down
pouring,
bending twigs,
flattening fern and leaf
and as suddenly,
stops.

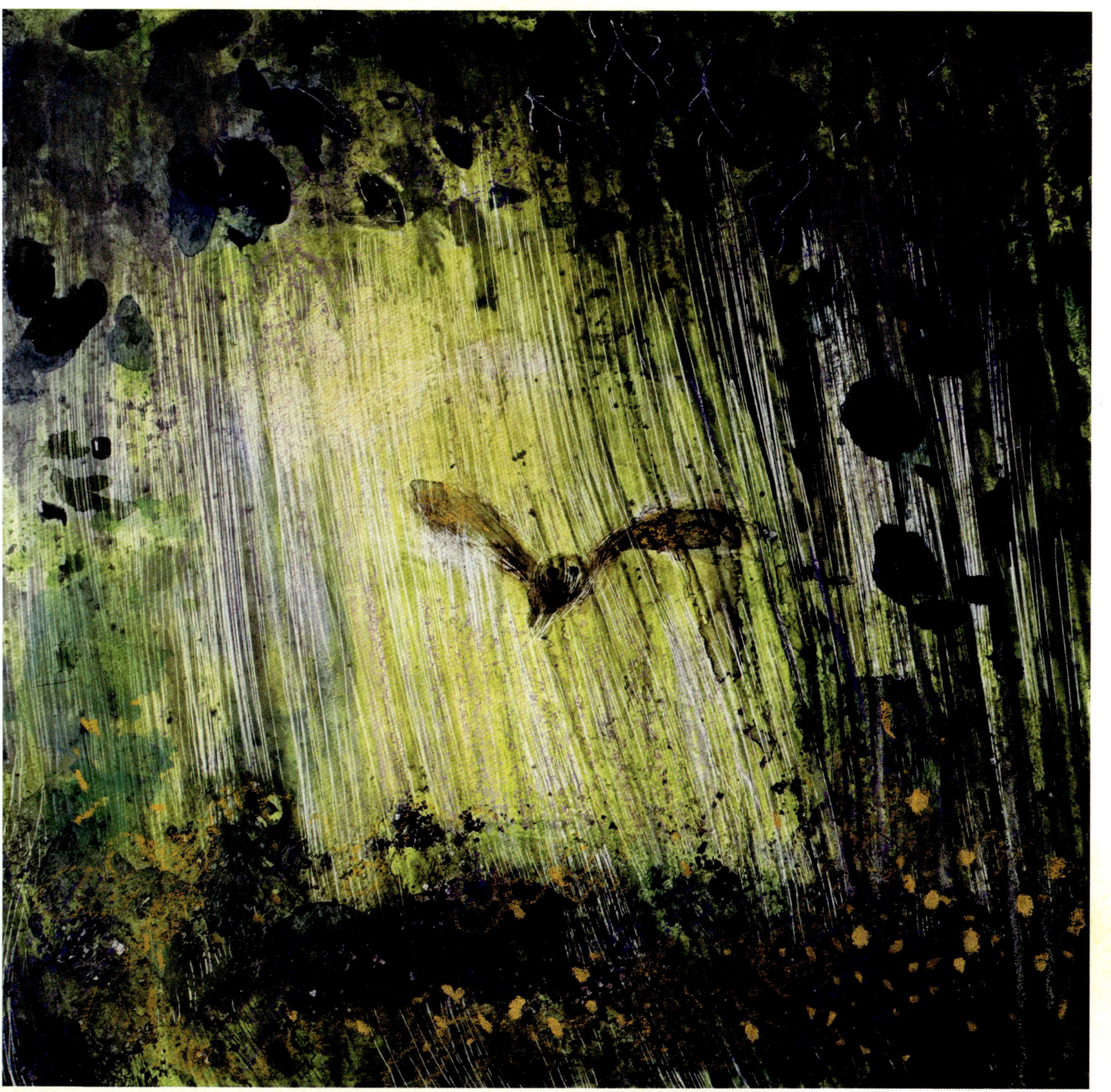

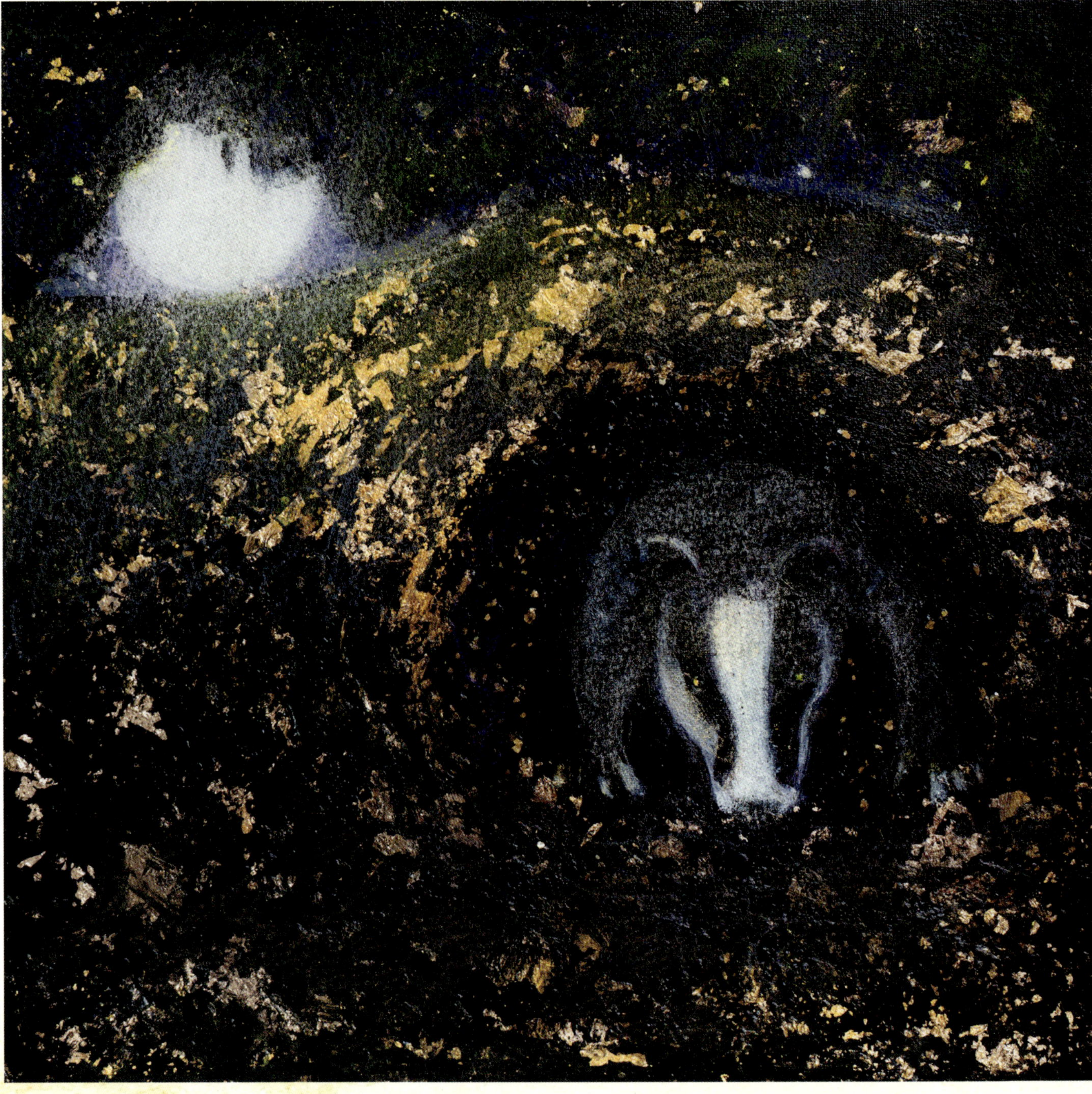

I hunt
under small oaks
where badger digs
his earthy nests
leaf and feather lined.
A rich garden:
brittle bones and mica,
crumblings of snail, centipedes and pale beetles.
He trundles on
crunching and sinking in the mulshy richness
questing nose snuffing grubs and worms.
Bear-like
through the woods,
and far beyond.

Does move,
mysterious
in the moon's path,
drinking from silvered puddles,
leaving delicate marks in wet earth,
traces of their passing.

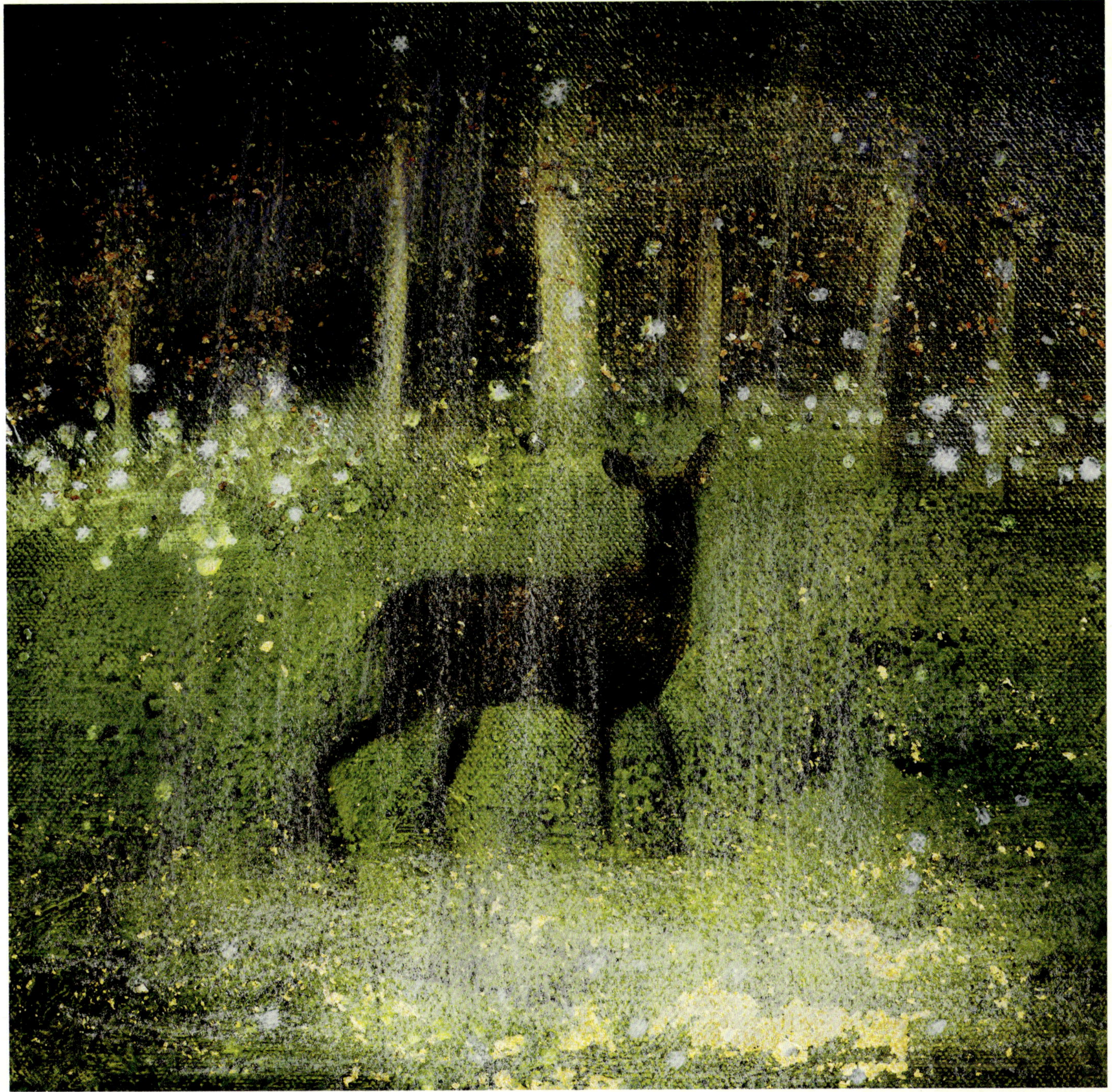

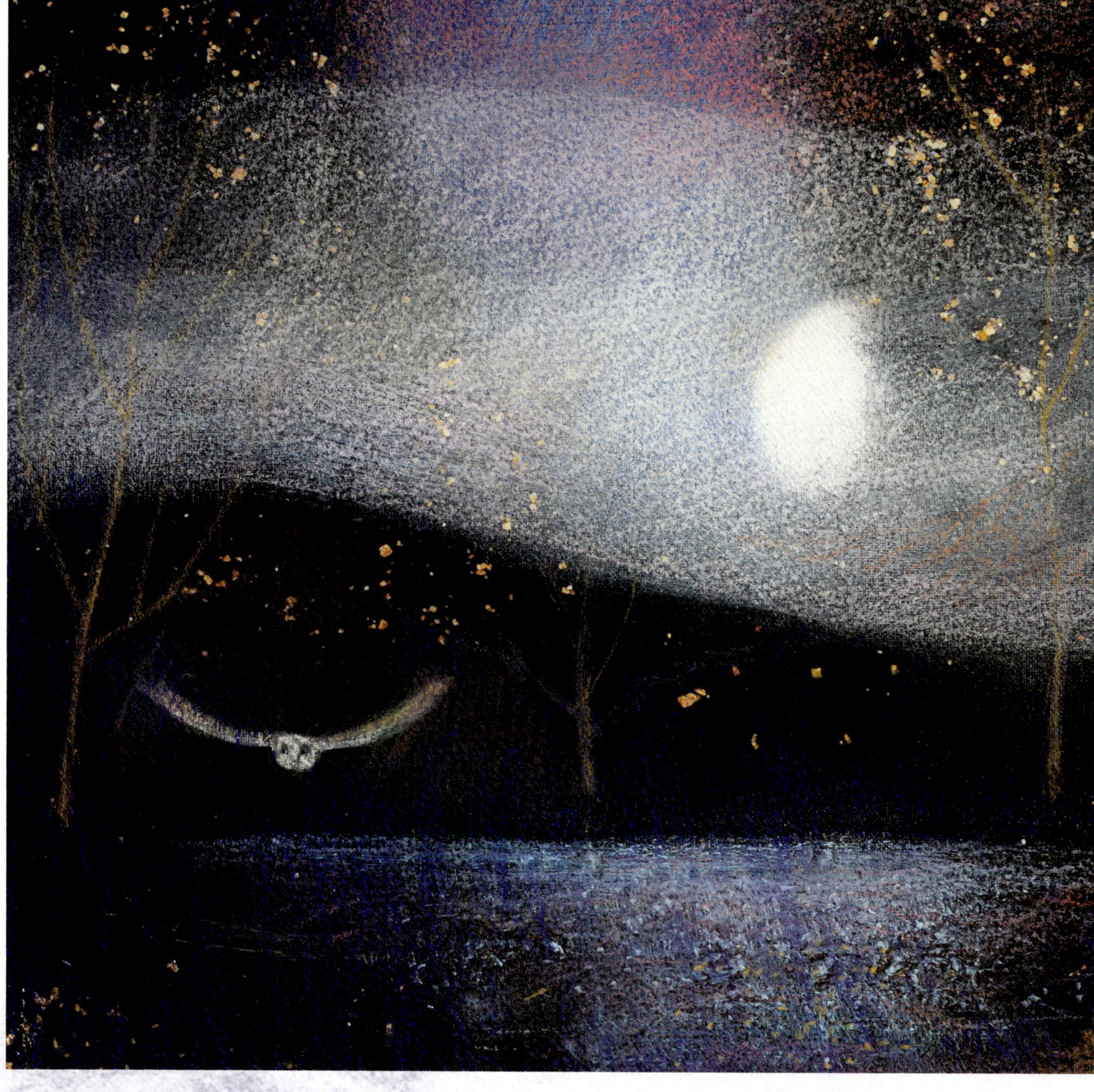

Mist rises.
Fox barks.

The wood waits.
Close,
she calls
Kee witt
Kee witt

I sit in my oak tree,
and I call darkling to me
I call owl light to me
I call dusk to me
I call twilight to me
I call the blue hour to me
I am Old Brown,
You know me.

Nearby,
she answers
Kee witt
Kee witt

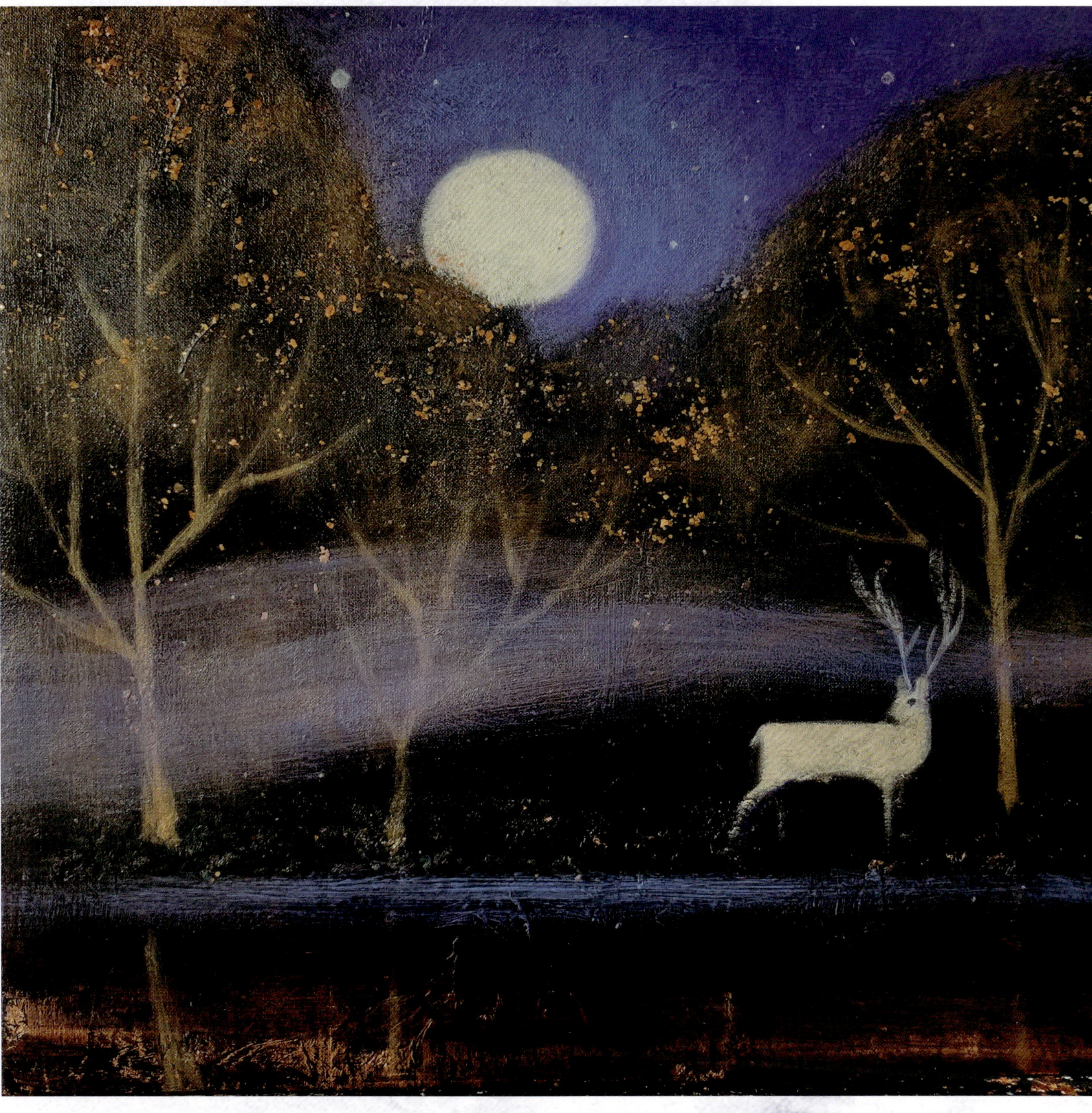

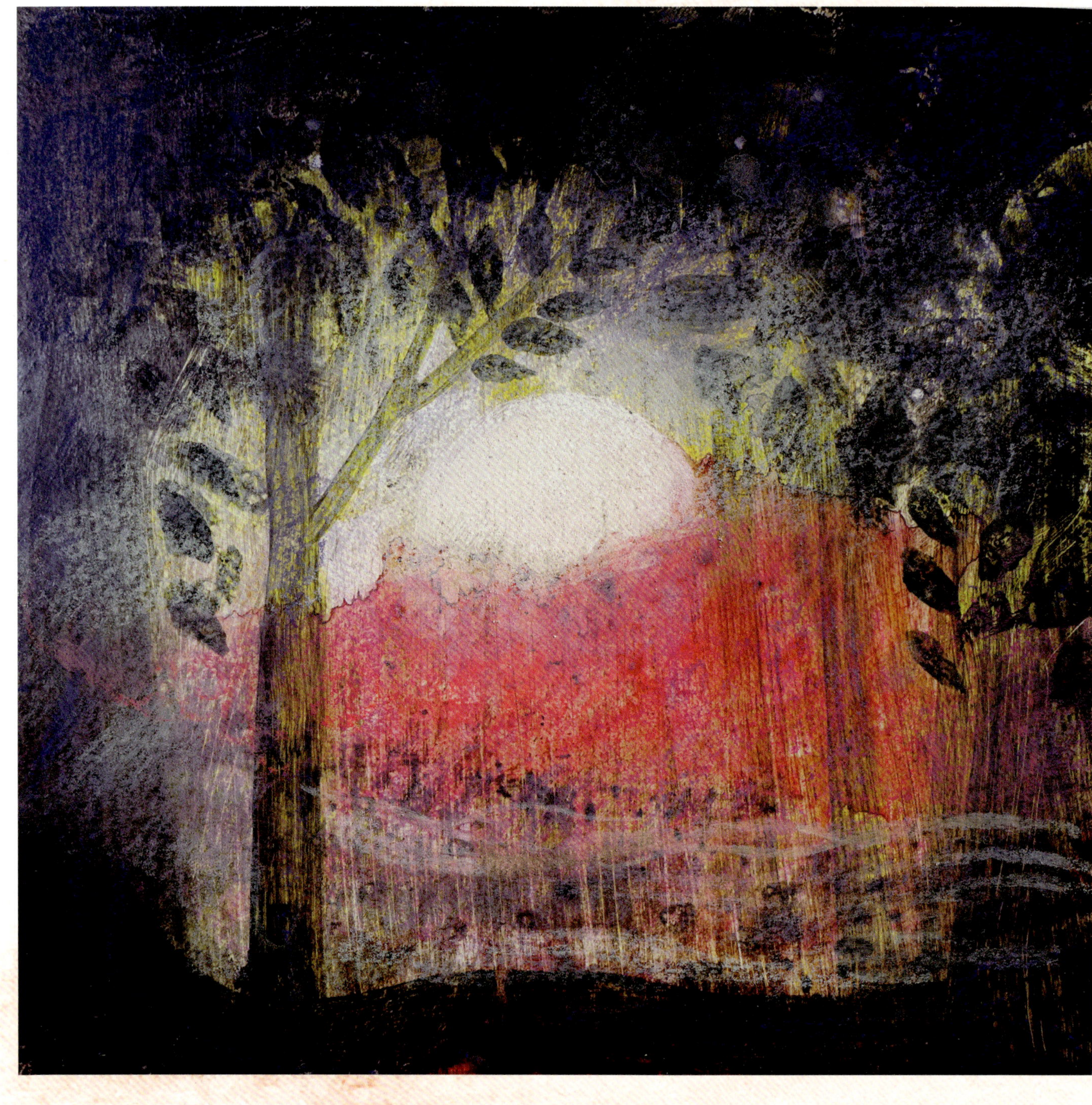

Mist creeps along river
as dawn's dew takes the night,
filling woodland hollows.

Stars melt above
where sleeping trees stir.

Earth tilts,
horizon glows.
The wild moon
hovers and
sinks.

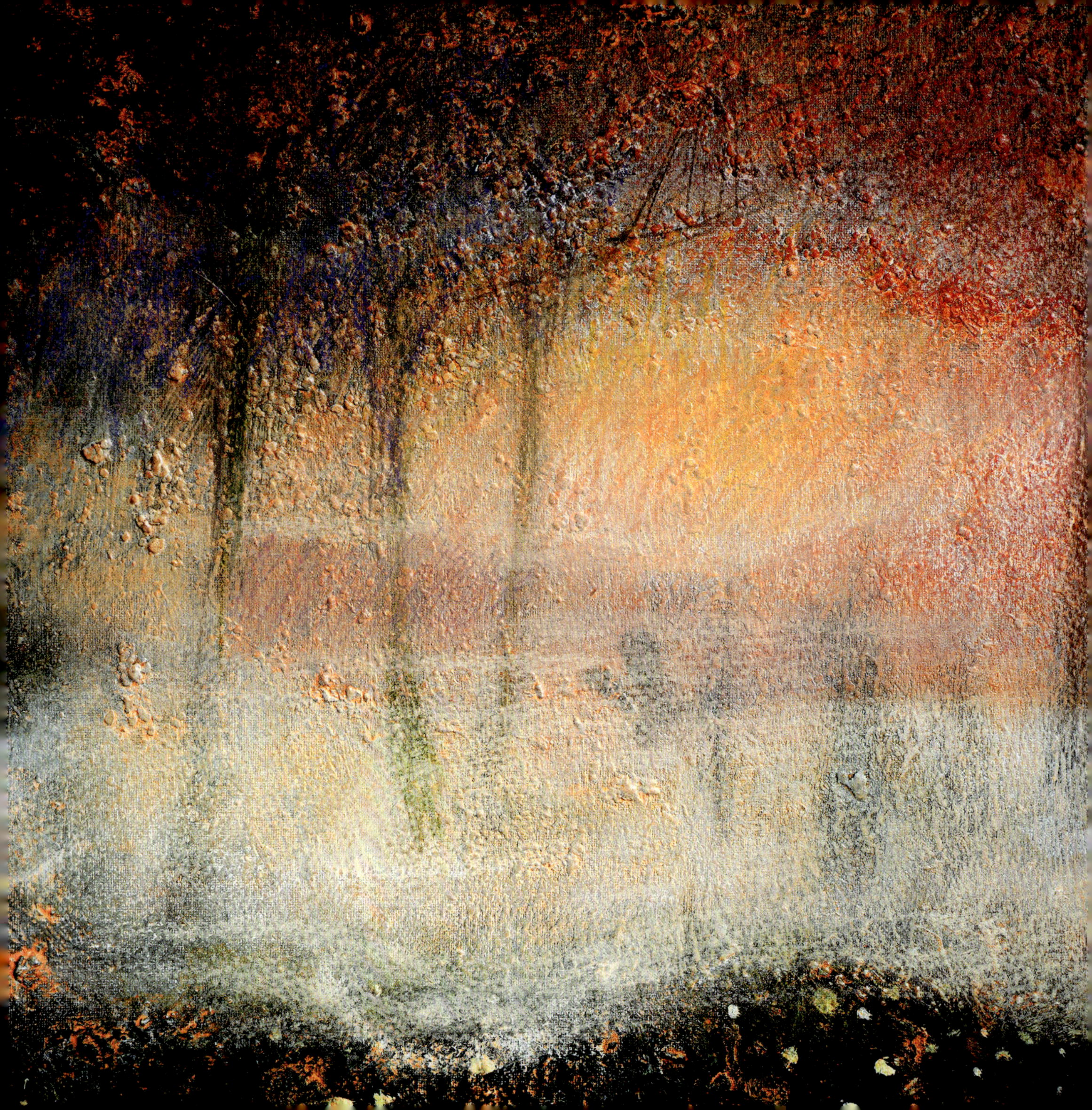

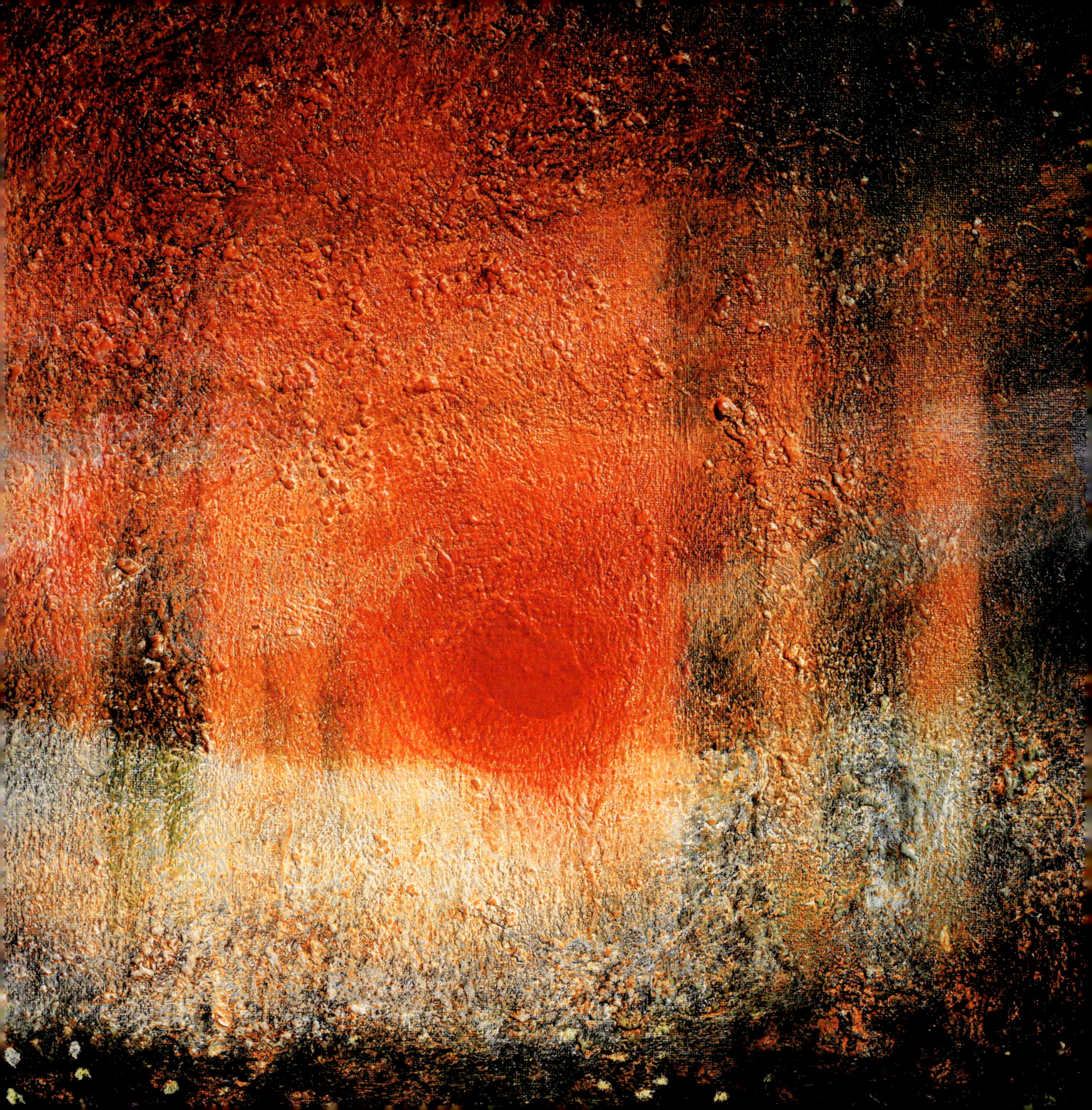

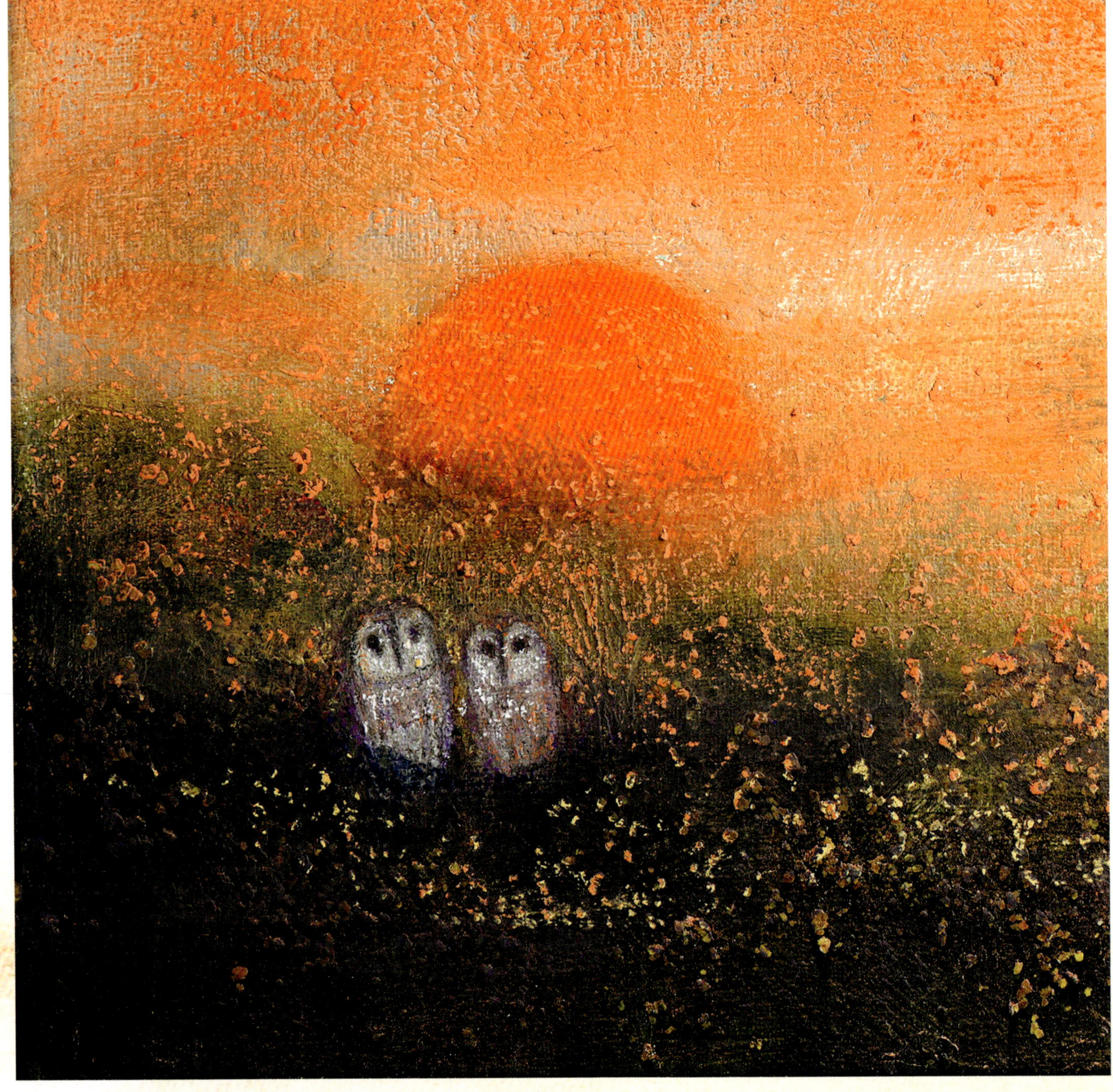

I call.
She answers.

Cockcrow.

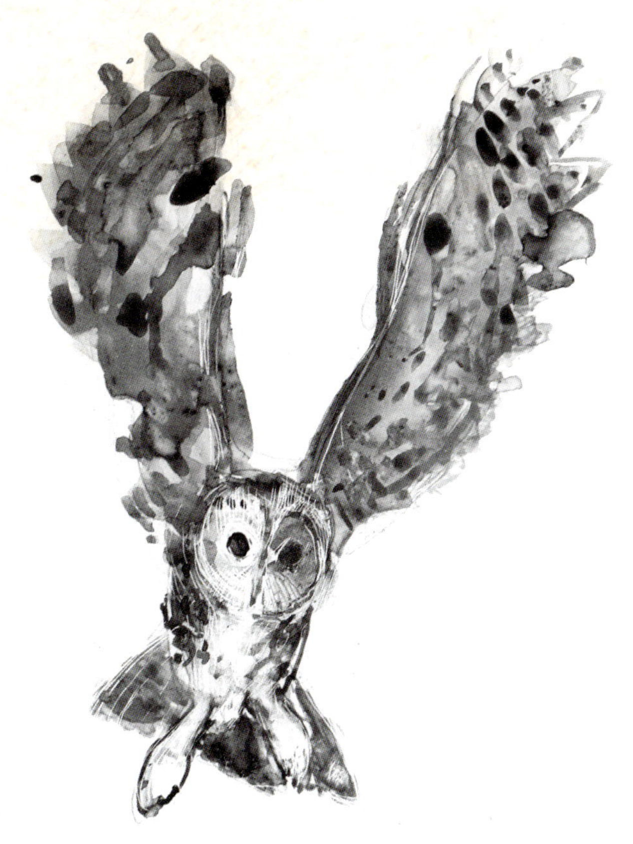

ABOUT *Artist & Poet*

CATHERINE HYDE

‘She is, if you will, a visual poet weaving images, symbols and archetypes into paintings that resonate in the subconscious and linger there like half-remembered dreams or the dark fairy stories with which she has such affiliation.’
Pip Palmer, *Galleries Magazine*

Artist and award-winning illustrator Catherine Hyde trained in Fine Art Painting at Central School of Art in London and exhibits and sells her atmospheric and symbolic work in galleries far and wide.

Catherine lives with her family in Cornwall, and works at the top of her house in her studio ‘in the sky’. *Darkling, The Owl’s Song* follows *The Bee and the Sun*, which won the Holyer an Gof Award in 2022 and its companion volume *The Hare and the Moon* published in 2019.